# LOVE ANYHOW

# Love Anyhow

## FAMOUS FATHERS WRITE

## TO THEIR CHILDREN

*Edited by Reid Sherline*

t TIMKEN PUBLISHERS

Published by Timken Publishers, Inc.
225 Lafayette Street, New York, NY 10012

LIBRARY OF CONGRESS CATALOGING-IN-PUBLICATION DATA
Love anyhow : famous fathers write to their children /
edited by Reid Sherline.
p.    cm.
ISBN 0-943221-19-6
1. Fathers—Correspondence.    2. Celebrities—
Correspondence.    3. Authors—Correspondence.
4. Father and child.    I. Sherline, Reid, date.
HQ756.L69        1994            94-1996 CIP
306.874'2—dc20

Type set in Galliard by Wilsted & Taylor
Designed by David Bullen
Copyedited by Anna Jardine

Printed in the United States of America

*For my father*

# CONTENTS

CONTENTS

## ON GOD AND RELIGION

## ON SEX, LOVE, AND MARRIAGE

## ON LIVING AND MISCELLANEOUS MATTERS

As old men love preaching, and I have some right to preach to you, I here present you with my sermon upon these words.

*Lord Chesterfield to his son, March 1751*

# INTRODUCTION

*Love Anyhow* began as a companion to *Letters Home: Celebrated Authors Write to Their Mothers.* The intention was for a small volume of letters from noted writers to their fathers. But after a quick look at source material, it became clear that the more compelling letters were not from children to their fathers but the reverse. Children to their fathers are often distant or defensive. They're businesslike, they want things (money more often than not). Fathers to their children are something else: their letters are a tightrope walk of hope and aspiration for youth, tempered by the disappointment and wisdom that come with age. Fathers tend also—perhaps unfortunately, though not surprisingly—to preach. They give advice, at every chance, on every imaginable subject—when their words are necessary, but also when they are not; when it seems likely they will be heard if not heeded, *and* when it is almost certain no one is home at the other end. Rather than resist fathers' tendencies to counsel and preach, I have chosen to surrender to them. So this volume consists of letters of advice, organized by subject, from mostly well-known fathers to their children.

The trouble with giving advice, of course, is that if one gives too much, some is bound to be bad. And good or bad, it is all colored by the giver's particular outlook and circumstances. For the editor attempting to assemble advice into a collection, the difficulty lies with the "bad" stuff. What about the wise words that prove to be not so wise after all? Or those that don't translate from another age into our own? A conventional book of fathers' wisdom might simply jettison what is bad or less than profound and leave pearls of wisdom of a line or two each. *Love Anyhow* takes another course: it leaves everything in. The pearls are here—but so are the clunkers. Advice, as these letters show, may be interesting, lively, poignant without being especially "good."

Indeed, the focus here is less words of wisdom per se than the unstated tensions between giver and receiver. For advice is communication, and as in any communication, there is a will on either end of it. Torn from context, it is aphorism; left in context, it allows something else to emerge. There is the voice of the giver, desirous, frustrated, fallible—human, in short. There is the receiver too, who sometimes resists and sometimes, cowed into silence, acquiesces.

I first noticed tension between giver and receiver of advice in Rainer Maria Rilke's *Letters to a Young Poet*. (These letters are not from a father to a son, but they might be.) I had read the letters once, in college, and had thought that everything in them was necessarily wise and true. When I read them again several years later, it occurred to me Rilke was not so much communicating with the student to whom his letters were addressed as he was attempting to reach across time to redeem some younger, sadder, more confused ghost of himself. Leo Tolstoy put it another way in one of the letters included in this collection: "I can't help being of the opinion that it's better not to marry if you can, in order to serve God with all your strength. But if you can't, you should marry and hand on what you haven't finished yourself to the children you bring into the world."

That is the key: A father's advice to his children, whether it is good or bad, is often the father's own unfinished business. This is true for Tolstoy, whose words to his son Lev on the subject of marriage—"fetter your freedom as little as possible"—appear an extension of Tolstoy's own regrets and unhappy experience in matrimony. And true also for F. Scott Fitzgerald admonishing his eleven-year-old daughter with a line from Shakespeare: "Lilies that fester smell far worse than weeds." It is hard to imagine that Fitzgerald was not referring to himself; here was a man who by his own admission had been "only a mediocre caretaker of most of the things left in [his] hands."

Not all the fathers included here are biological (there are a godfather and a spiritual father). And contrary to the book's subtitle, not all of them are famous. A woman looking to these pages for useful words of wisdom will no doubt be disappointed. On the whole, daughters have a rough time of it; with few exceptions, they are told to dress nicely and deport themselves so they will make good, if not beautiful, wives. The fathers are not entirely at fault in this. After all, no words of wisdom were ever uttered in a vacuum, and the words that follow were all written by fathers who lived in a specific place and time. Fathers today—one hopes—tell their daughters different things. In other respects, however, things have changed remarkably little over the centuries. Whether it is 1715 or 1994, fathers want their children to be clean; they want them to do well in school; they want them to be happy and successful in life.

The purpose of *Love Anyhow* is to draw advice from the vague space of universality where we tend to keep it and insert it into the landscape of particulars from which it emerged. This is fathers' advice not for the sake of advice but rather for the sake of fathers and their children. Fatherly love should be taken as it comes—and that, more often than not, is as exhortation and admonishment, with an added burden of expectation and unfinished business.

# Love

# Anyhow

# ON EDUCATION

By the time he retired from public life, at the age of fifty-three, Philip Dormer Stanhope (1694–1773), the fourth Earl of Chesterfield, had been ambassador to the Hague, lord lieutenant of Ireland, and secretary of state to the Foreign Office. He also had fathered a child, a boy—named Philip, after himself—who was born out of wedlock in 1732.

Chesterfield's many letters of advice to his son are famous. First published in 1774, the letters have been in and out of print ever since (a selection was reissued as recently as 1989). They were written during the younger Philip's education, his grand tour of Europe, and throughout his career as a politician. Elected twice to Parliament, he also held several diplomatic positions; he died when he was thirty-six.

As well known as Lord Chesterfield is for dispensing advice, he is by no means beyond reproach. He has been accused of, among other things, being a man with "the mien of a posture-maker . . . who affects the supercilious air of a shallow dandy and cherishes the heart of a frog."

It is tempting to read Lord Chesterfield's letters to his son as more than advice on how to live as a gentleman; they also offer a detailed strategy by which Philip might rise above his illegitimacy.

◆ ◆ ◆

*December 1747*

Dear Boy,

Remember that whatever knowledge you do not solidly lay the foundation of before you are eighteen, you will never be master of while you breathe. Knowledge is a comfortable and necessary retreat and shelter for us in an advanced age; and if we do not plant it while young, it will give us no shade when we grow old. I neither require nor expect from you great application to books after you are once thrown out into the great world. I know it is impossible; and it may even, in some cases, be improper: this, therefore, is your time, and your only time, for unwearied and uninterrupted application. If you should sometimes think it a little laborious, consider the labour is the unavoidable fatigue of a necessary journey. The more hours a day you travel, the sooner you will be at your journey's end. The sooner you are qualified for your liberty, the sooner you shall have it; and your manumission will entirely depend upon the manner in which you employ the intermediate time. I think I offer you a very good bargain, when I promise you, upon my word, that, if you will do everything that I would have you do till you are eighteen, I will do everything that you would have me do ever afterwards.

I knew a gentleman, who was so good a manager of time, that he would not even lose that small portion of which the calls of nature obliged him to pass in the necessary-house, but gradually went through all the Latin poets in those moments. He bought, for example, a common edition of Horace, of which he tore off gradually a couple of pages, carried them with him to that necessary place, read them first, and then sent them down as a sacrifice to Cloacina; this was so much time fairly gained; and I recommend to you to follow his example. It is better than only doing what you cannot help doing at those moments; and it will make any book which you shall read in that manner, very present to your mind. Books of science, and of a grave sort, must be read with continuity; but there are very many, and even very useful ones, which may be read with advantage by snatches, and unconnectedly; such are all the good Latin poets, except Virgil in his Æneid: and such are most of the modern poets in which you will find many pieces worth reading that will not take up above seven or eight minutes. Bayle's, Moreri's, and other dictionaries, are proper books to take and shut up for the little intervals of (otherwise) idle time, that everybody has in the course of the day, between either their studies or their pleasures. Good night!

# SAMUEL TAYLOR COLERIDGE
*to his son Derwent*

*A shadow hung over Samuel Taylor Coleridge's (1772–1834) second son, Derwent, when he started at Cambridge in 1821: the year before, his older brother, Hartley, had been expelled from Oxford. The accusations against Hartley—that he was intemperate and, in the words of the college authorities, "fond of society very different from that of his own Common Room, and by no means respectable"—were particularly distressing to his father.*

*Coleridge worried about Derwent; he worried that his second son would follow the bad example set by his first. When news reached him that Derwent's excellent academic standing had slipped slightly, he assumed the worst. He imagined for his son a life of "extra-academic Society, Concerts, Balls." "Is dissipation of mind and spirit," he asks in the letter that follows, "the fit recreation of a Student?" To Derwent's reassuring reply, Coleridge wrote, "I am glad to be able to correct my fears as far as public balls, concerts, and time-murder in Narcissism." That Coleridge should accuse his son in this manner is ironic; he himself had never finished his education at Cambridge and was addicted to opium.*

*Derwent's behavior continued to vex his father. He quit Cambridge and refused to take orders as Coleridge wanted. Eventually, however, he came around, returning to the university, abandoning his atheism, and agreeing to enter the church.*

◆ ◆ ◆

*11 Jany. 1822.*

My dear Derwent

I sit with my pen only not touching the paper, and my head hanging over it; but *what* to write and with what purpose I write at all, I know not. What can I urge that would not be the mere repetition of counsels already urged with

all the weight that my earnest intreaties could add to them, so often both before you went to Cambridge and since? What that would not be the echo of
echoes, which of late have *volleyed* round you in a circle—admonitions
which Friends of all ages, of your own & even your Juniors have given you—
and I trust, that wisest and most faithful of all Friends, your own Conscience?
To study to the injury of your health, and the undermining of your Consti-
tution—was *this* required of you? You have long known both my judgment
and my wishes in this respect: that a Senior Wranglership with the first Classical Medal as it's Appendage would be a poor compensation to *me* and in *my*
thoughts for shattered nerves and diseased digestive organs. You cannot do
without intermissions of Study, without recreation and such as society only
can afford you—?—Be it so! But is dissipation of mind and spirit the fit recreation of a Student? Or not rather the fever fit, of which your Studies are like
to be the cold, feeble and languid Intermittents? 'I have known instances of
Drinkers and Whore-mongers', said Mr Montague to me a few weeks [ago];
'but in all my long experience of Cambridge never did I see or hear of any one
instance of a high Wrangler with or without classical honors, who was a man
of Pleasure, Dress, and Family Visiting.' Even extra-collegiate Society, by
preference & in a larger proportion than that of his own college, and the flar-
ing about with distinguished Graduates &c; never yet made even if it left a
man friends in his own College—who are after all from obvious causes the
friends most likely to stick by us. But extra-academic Society, Concerts,
Balls—Dressing, and an hour and a half or two Hours not seldom devoted
to so respectable a purpose—O God!—even the disappointment as to your
success in the university, mortifying as I feel it, arising from such causes and
morally ominous, as it becomes in your particular case & with the claims,
that *you* must recognize on your exertions, is not the worst. This accursed
Coxcombry, like Daeianira's gift, sends a ferment into the very Life-blood of
a Young man's Sense and Genius—and ends in a schirrus of the Heart.—I
know by experience what the social recreation is that does an undergraduate
good. In my first Term, and from October till March, I read hard and system-

atically. I had no acquaintance, much less suitable, (i.e.) studious, Companion in my own College. Six nights out of seven, as soon as chapel was over, I went to Pembroke, to Middleton's (the present B. of Calcutta) Rooms—opened the door without speaking, made and poured out the Tea and placed his cup beside his Book—went on with my Æschylus or Thucydides, as he with his Mathematics, in silence till ½ past 9—then closed our books at the same moment—the size and college Ale came in—& till 12 we had true Noctes atticae which I cannot to this hour think of without a strong emotion—. With what delight did I not resume my reading in my own Rooms at Jesus [College] each following Morning. Think you a Ball or a Concert or a Lady Party, or a Literary Club, would have left me in the same state—and your studies mathematical? Were it possible even that it could be otherwise—yet your character must suffer. If from Ill-health or any other cause, should your (I quote Middleton's sweet Sonnet to me)

> young Ambition feel the wound
> Of blighted Hope and Laurels sought in vain—

what sort of *solution* will be the one current? He *trifled* away his success!—Can you not controll your Love of appearance and Showing off for two or three years? At the end of that time the very qualities that indulged in the interval will stamp you a trifler &, with such claims on you, far worse! would be construed into merit by the major part of the world—as not too learned to be agreeable &c &c. . . .

I am not angry, Derwent!—but it is calamitous that you do not know how anxiously & affectionately I am your *Father*—

*S. T. Coleridge*

P.S. I hear that you are Premier or Secretary of a Literary Club—about old books.—If such things did not dissipate your time & thoughts, they *dissipate* and perplex your *character*—They are well enough for B.A.s & M.A.s—

# RUDYARD KIPLING *to his daughter Elsie*

*"His genius," Elliot Gilbert says of Rudyard Kipling (1865–1936) in his introduction to* "O Beloved Kids": Rudyard Kipling's Letters to his Children, *"was . . . to be the father of children; his tragedy was to be deprived of them and permanently scarred by their departure." Indeed, Kipling cherished his role as father; sadly, however, of his three children, only one, Elsie, lived to be an adult.*

*Josephine, Kipling's oldest child, died at age seven, of pneumonia (the same illness that almost killed Kipling himself). John, the youngest—and Kipling's only son—died in combat in 1915, six weeks after his eighteenth birthday. In her memoir Elsie writes: "The two great sorrows of their lives my parents bore bravely and silently."*

*As his letters to Elsie and John attest, the author of* Just So Stories *and the* Jungle Books *was no ordinary Edwardian paterfamilias but, in the words of Gilbert, a man "who [brought] up his young son and daughter with imagination, tenderness, comic exuberance, deep affection, and the lightest possible touch."*

*The letter that follows, written to Elsie when she was seventeen, is one of few from Kipling to his daughter that survive from this period. Most are to John, who was away at school; there are, however, hundreds of letters that Kipling wrote Elsie after John's death and her own marriage. Elsie served as her father's literary executor until her death in 1977.*

◆ ◆ ◆

*Hotel Regina, Paris.*
*[February 5, 1913] 8.45 p.m.*

*Very dear Daughter,*

It seems about one year and a half since you went away—and that is why I sit down—I mean to say stand up at the mantelpiece to tell you how we love you. By this time I expect you will have met the other maidens and found them mildly interesting specimens of a breed of which you do not know much— the British Female Girl. In eight and forty hours you should be as thick as thieves together, and when the time comes for your return you'll grieve to be separated from them. Mother, who is going to bed, here interpolates that she has found a pair of nail scissors which you left behind but as she knows you have another pair and as these happen to be handy she intends to hang on to 'em. In other words, she says, she does not know how to get them to you.

I won't burden you with advice. I know you will be good: but what I want you to do is be interested in your companions and your surroundings. Up to now you haven't had many companions, and you have regulated your sur-roundings to suit yourself. Now, my darling, you're in the world for a little bit on your own and (here's the whole secret of life) as you treat the world so will it treat you. Your esteemed parents do *not* treat you as you treat them but the world, which is chiefly busy with its own concerns, behaves otherwise. If you smile at the world, it grins. If you frown at it, it scowls. This is knowledge that you will learn before a week is out. I merely mention it that you may rec-ognize it when it comes along. Selah!

Now I want you to write your little brother at Wellington a full true and particular account (much fuller than you'd write to *us*) of your feelings and experiences in your new life. *He'*ll understand because, you see, he goes out into the cold hard world three times a year—and also he remembers what his first day at school was like. Tell him fully and you'll find that he'll sympathize with you no end and that you'll have another bond of sympathy between you.

And I think that's all. We're going to bed (I hope you are there already!) Mother finds that the new feather in her new hat is insecurely placed and she is giving it a new "security". Gawd knows whether "security" means tintacks or resewing it but it makes her happy. Now she is in the scantiest of attire, lecturing away as she undresses. I will spare you a picture and I will subscribe myself

*Ever and ever*
*Your most loving Pater*

# EUGENE O'NEILL *to his son Eugene Jr.*

*Eugene O'Neill (1888–1953) was twenty-one—a long way from the four Pulitzer Prizes and the Nobel he was to win—when his first child was born. His marriage to the boy's mother, Kathleen Jenkins, had been arranged hastily; afterward O'Neill's parents, who did not approve of the match, shipped him off—just as hastily—to Honduras. The next three years were turbulent and unhappy: he traveled extensively, divorced his wife, attempted suicide once, and by the end of 1912 contracted tuberculosis.*

*O'Neill was far closer to Eugene Jr., who was born of this early tumult, than to Shane and Oona, the children from his second marriage to Agnes Boulton, who were born during his initial success as a playwright. He admitted in a letter to Eugene, "Well, my trying to have any influence on the two of them [Shane and Oona] was foolish. The dice were loaded. I felt that all the time."*

*Apparently Eugene Jr. took to heart his father's advice to "get something worth [his] while" out of his years at Yale. After a fruitful undergraduate career, he became a faculty member in classics there. He published scholarly articles and coedited a two-volume* Complete Greek Drama. *(His father's formal education had ended when he was dismissed from Princeton after his freshman year.)*

*Like his father in other ways, though, Eugene Jr. did not enjoy personal triumph. His three marriages were troubled. He left Yale to enter radio and television broadcasting, and began to drink heavily. In September 1950, after his third divorce and many aimless years of drinking, he committed suicide. He was forty years old.*

◆ ◆ ◆

*(c/o Guaranty Trust Co., 50, Pall Mall, London)*
*(you'd better use this address as I'm leaving here soon)*
*[early September 1928]*

*Dear Eugene:*

Hope you got my cable all right. Consider it a lazy man's letter. Or, more kindly, a busy man's—for it's no lie to say I've been, and still am, busy getting *Dynamo* finished and typed and gone over so I can submit it to the Guild at the earliest possible moment. I expect now to have it mailed to them in about a week. Then will come a breathing spell which I'll be glad to reach for I'm dead tired and my brain is like a wrung sponge. The last part of *Dynamo* has been intensive work, there was so much to jam into such small space. The concentrated medium of the drama takes it out of one at such times. Well, at any rate, the play is written now and I feel it's "one of the ones," in spite of the usual reaction after a thing is finished of its seeming like a lot of junk.

Did I say I'd enjoy a breathing spell soon? Well, not so damn soon. There's packing and moving out of here and a million odds and ends to attend to. I won't really be able to sit back and rest until I get on the boat for China the first week in October.

Yes, I'm going to the Far East—sailing for Hong Kong and way stations the first week in October. I expect to spend some time in China, then go to Java and India for more or less short periods. After that—but here my plans are indefinite. It all depends on how things work out. I may go down the African coast and spend a couple of months in the Transvaal and Rhodesia. I've got to pick out a place in the East for two months' work and another place later on for another two months. The rest of the time will be given to travel. I'll be back here in France by the first of July at the latest. And, if you want to, I want you to plan to come over next summer and stay with me in this Basque country and see a lot of France (and Europe in general if you want to make trips around on your own). I'm planning now to make my permanent home here, once it's time to settle down again. I feel more at home here than I've ever felt anywhere before—more at peace and "belonging," even though I don't speak the language much. By the way, for Pete's sake go in a bit for French in the meantime. You'll be missing a lot if you don't—and there's no reason why you shouldn't come over here any summer you like from now on.

One reason I'm deciding to settle here is, of course, financial. You can live so much better here on so much less money.

I hope that by next spring all this present "hold-out" policy of Agnes's will be settled. If it isn't, well I know the situation here will be taken for granted by you. The didacs of a revengeful wife cannot be helped, I suppose—and may be expected, until she gets tired of being a bum sport. But, I sure hope to be divorced and remarried by then.

I hope you're going to like Yale and get something worth your while out of it. Enjoy your life there—that's the main thing (this sounds like all hell in the way of advice from a father!)—but give a thought once in a while to what you want to do with your life after college and, since you've got to work to stick there, try to give your work (your choice of it) some definite direction toward some goal. And do go out strong for that crew! I think the spirit one gets out of college athletics is a damn fine thing—provided, of course, one has the brains and character to keep the athlete part of one in its place, which you have. I've felt all my life that that was one value in life I cheated myself out of by my own perverse cussedness. I am under no illusions that I could ever have been a shining star at anything but it would have done me a hell of a lot of good inside—not to add, physically—if I had put myself through the self-discipline of trying to be. All of which sounds a bit confused. But you get me.

Another bit of brotherly—(for I always feel in such matters as if you were more a young brother than a son)—caution I want to hand you about college out of my fund of experience with college men is this: Don't get out of your own financial depth in the fellows you chum with. Nothing tends to have a worse effect on character than this (see all the psychologists!). I don't mean by this to avoid the rich because they're rich—as a matter of fact it's sons from families who have had money for generations who get along on moderate spending money—it's the heirs of the nouveaus who splurge. You know about what my status is—an up and down one with one flush year followed by one or two lean ones. For example, this year is grand while last year I was paying for Spithead [O'Neill's Bermuda home] and living on (mostly) the sale of securities that I'd bought when *Desire* [*Under the Elms*] was going strong. Perhaps I'm due for more continuous good luck in the future. I hope so—but you never can tell. The theatre, financially speaking, is always a gamble.

But I don't want you to think I'm crying poor. I have the deepest faith in your balance and good sense (which you can thank your Mother for as you certainly didn't get that virtue from me!) and I want you to know that anything you feel you need you can certainly have, without question, as long as I can give it to you. And you must feel it's your right to ask for it. You've got to come forward and not be modest. It will make it a lot easier for me. You see, it's a hell of a while since I went to college and I have no friends with sons there, so I'm completely out of touch with the current values of modern undergraduate life. I want you, as my son and for the sake of your own development in the four years, to hold up your end on your own proper level simply and with breeding and dignity. To give a sort of indicative example which may be revealing to you: I want you to have one fine, perfectly-fitting expensive suit of clothes where others will have three maybe but each minus the distinction. It will be less expensive for you & you'll be better dressed. This sounds like What the W. D. Man should W. but I'm no bug on clothes. The same dope goes for everything.

That being off my chest, let me say how proud I was you came off so well in the entrance exams. Keep up the good work. There is one aspect of college on which I have drastically changed my mind since I graced (at least "graced" is part of the word the Dean used, if I remember!) the campus of Old Nassau and that is the notion that one must not, under any compulsion, learn anything there. I believe now that it is rather good dope, and helps one to enjoy life, if one *does learn* as much as one can.

I'm enclosing a check to your Mother. This is extra, tell her, to use to help you in your first half term in any way you decide best between you. The usual check will, of course, be forthcoming, via Harry [O'Neill's lawyer], the first of year. You can read her what I've said about college etc. and if she vetoes any of my "advice," consider it vetoed. She has more sense than I will ever have.

Write me your impressions of Old Eli after you've been there a bit. Call on Baker and William Lyon Phelps and President Angell and tell them who you are. It may help—if my Yale Litt.D. counts for anything. They are all fine men and you'll like them. Also if you ever happen near William Brown, Dean of the Divinity School, introduce yourself. He was my sponsor that day. I think he expected to find me (being a divine) a cross between a gunman and the devil and was most edified by my surprising knowledge of theology and early Christianity (from the reading I'd done for *Lazarus*). But I liked him and think he liked me.

I'm sending you my itinerary for the trip—but you better always use c/o Guaranty Trust Co., 50, Pall Mall, London as address as I'll keep cabling them any change in plan and exact dates my whereabouts. Also Harry will know. Give your Mother Harry's address. Go to him in any sudden emergency.

And that's about all, I guess. I'll write you anything of interest from the East. I expect to get a lot from it as spiritual background for my future life and work. It's always called to me. When I was a sailor I was always aiming for there but never made it.

Be good and be happy! Give me a thought once in a while. I'm really profoundly proud and fond of you—after my fashion which is inarticulate about such things—and I know there is a rare feeling between us that ought to make both our lives richer as the years go by.

*All love to you always!*
*Your Father*

# F. SCOTT FITZGERALD
*to his daughter Frances*

---

*The thirties were not easy years for F. Scott Fitzgerald (1896–1940). The Great Depression was on. His wife, Zelda, spent the better part of the decade in and out of hospitals, after suffering three nervous breakdowns. Fitzgerald himself was drinking too much. And his writing career, on a downhill slide since the 1925 publication of* The Great Gatsby, *was a shambles.*

*He and Zelda had one child, a daughter named Frances, whom Fitzgerald sent away—first to camp, and later to the Ethel Walker School in Troy, New York. He wanted to keep her insulated, at a safe distance from a depression that was in every way both national and personal. Not surprisingly some of his own disappointment and bitterness crept into the letters he sent her during this period. In the two that follow, Fitzgerald's tone fluctuates, from doting to prickly, and his advice is often far from a child's concerns. He warns his daughter with Shakespeare: "Lilies that fester smell far worse than weeds." He tells her that "to justify [her] inheritance" she must "accept the sadness, the tragedy of the world we live in with a certain esprit." Yet running through all is his fierce love for her—and hope for her—in the face of his own terrible ruin.*

◆ ◆ ◆

*La Paix, Rodger's Forge,*
*Towson, Maryland*
*August 8, 1933*

*Dear Pie:*

I feel very strongly about you doing [your] duty. Would you give me a little more documentation about your reading in French? I am glad you are happy—but I never believe much in happiness. I never believe in misery either. Those are things you see on the stage or the screen or the printed page, they never really happen to you in life.

All I believe in in life is the rewards for virtue (according to your talents) and the *punishments* for not fulfilling your duties, which are doubly costly. If there is such a volume in the camp library, will you ask Mrs. Tyson to let you look up a sonnet of Shakespeare's in which the line occurs *"Lilies that fester smell far worse than weeds."*

Have had no thoughts today, life seems composed of getting up a *Saturday Evening Post* story. I think of you, and always pleasantly; but if you call me "Pappy" again I am going to take the White Cat out and beat his bottom *hard, six times for every time you are impertinent.* Do you react to that?

I will arrange the camp bill.

Half-wit, I will conclude.


Things to worry about:

    Worry about courage

    Worry about cleanliness

    Worry about efficiency

    Worry about horsemanship

    Worry about . . .

Things not to worry about:

    Don't worry about popular opinion

    Don't worry about dolls

    Don't worry about the past

    Don't worry about the future

    Don't worry about growing up

    Don't worry about anybody getting ahead of you

    Don't worry about triumph

    Don't worry about failure unless it comes through your own fault

    Don't worry about mosquitoes

Don't worry about flies
Don't worry about insects in general
Don't worry about parents
Don't worry about boys
Don't worry about disappointments
Don't worry about pleasures
Don't worry about satisfactions

Things to think about:

What am I really aiming at?

How good am I really in comparison to my contemporaries in regard to:

(a) Scholarship

(b) Do I really understand about people and am I able to get along with them?

(c) Am I trying to make my body a useful instrument or am I neglecting it?

*With dearest love,*
*[Daddy]*

P.S. My come-back to your calling me Pappy is christening you by the word Egg, which implies that you belong to a very rudimentary state of life and that I could break you up and crack you open at my will and I think it would be a word that would hang on if I ever told it to your contemporaries. "Egg Fitzgerald." How would you like that to go through life with—"Eggie Fitzgerald" or "Bad Egg Fitzgerald" or any form that might occur to fertile minds? Try it once more and I swear to God I will hang it on you and it will be up to you to shake it off. Why borrow trouble?

*Love anyhow.*

*November 10, 1936*
*Grove Park Inn*
*Asheville, N. C.*

*Dearest Pie:*

I got a School letter about Thanksgiving saying that Thanksgiving day is best, and it is much better for me that way. There is no particular advantage in going out two or three times rather than one, without any particular objectives; the idea is to go out once and have a good time. I will be delighted to meet Agnes, and our engagement is on Thanksgiving day.

Now, this is a parenthesis in my letter: I got the little charms that you sent me for my birthday: the bells dangling from the string and the mule, and I appreciated your thought of me—in a reverse way, you little donkey.

Park Avenue girls are hard, aren't they? My own taste ran to kinder people, but they are usually the daughters of "up-and-coming" men and, in a way, the inevitable offspring of that type. It is the Yankee push to its last degree, a sublimation of the sort of Jay Gould who began by peddling buttons to a country and ended with the same system of peddler's morals by peddling railroads to a nation.

Don't mistake me. I think of myself always as a Northerner and I think of you as a Northerner. Nevertheless, we are all one nation now and you will find all the lassitude and laziness that you despise among those girls, enough to fill Savannah and Charleston, just as down here you will find the same "go getter" principle in the Carolinas.

About the happy medium—which usually means to establish a state of happiness that has happened before and may possibly, under favorable circumstances, happen again; you have got to throw yourself one way or another, that is to say, you have got to say that I am dedicated to a scholastic life for the moment, or I am going to play around. Knowing your wise moderation in all things, I am not presuming to give your [*sic*] advice in this matter, except such advice as we can all take, whether we are Eleanor Turnbulls or Monseigneur Voltaires.

If you really were a happy medium you would probably be the most popular girl in school, which is the last thing I would want of you. I would like you to be a defiant little point of light at the end of a diamond, and if you have fools to be with, to make them a setting.

I don't know whether you will stay there another year—it all depends on your marks and your work, and I can't give you the particular view of life that I have, which as you know is a tragic one, without dulling your enthusiasm. A whole lot of people have found it a whole lot of fun. I have not found it so. But, my God, I had a hell of a lot of fun when I was in my twenties and thirties; and I feel that your duty to justify your inheritance is to accept the sadness, the tragedy of the world we live in with a certain *esprit*.

You have seen the shallowness of the Park Avenue girls, but if you had gone to school down here you would have seen the sort of half-ass attitude with which Southern women accept the decay of their race and cowardice of their men.

Now, insofar as your course is concerned, there is no question of your dropping mathematics and taking the easiest way to go into Vassar and being one of the girls fitted for nothing except to reflect other people without having any particular character of your own. I want you to take mathematics up to the limit of what the school offers. I want you to take physics and I want you to take chemistry. I don't care a damn about your English courses or your French courses. If you don't know two languages and the ways that great men chose to express their thoughts in those languages by this time, then you are not my daughter. You have got to do something hard and tough before you justify yourself with me entirely. You are an only child, but that doesn't give you any freedom of consonance with egotism.

*I want you to know certain basic scientific principles,* and I feel that is impossible to learn unless you have the schooling of an East side newsboy or that of a scholar who has gone as far into mathematics and its inevitable results as coordinate geometry. I don't want you to give up mathematics next year. I learned about writing from doing something that I didn't have any taste for. If you don't carry your mathematics such as coordinate geometry (conic sections—or they may have some new name for it now) up to the point of calculus, you will have strayed far afield from what I had planned for you. If you don't care to carry beyond the calculus, it will show in the result of what struggles you may have with it; but you are not planning your course of study. I am doing that for the moment. Whether or not you make a success of it is my business and yours, but it is nothing to be decided by what is easiest. I have put too much thought into your education for that. You are going into Vassar with mathematical credits and a certain side of your life there is going to be scientific, and, as I used to say, it is not a subject of discussion: it is simply what I wish.

Honey, I wish I could see you. It would be so much easier to go over these important matters without friction, but at a distance it seems rather tough that you are inclined to take the easiest way and slide into the subjects that are easy for you, like languages.

No more until I see you Thanksgiving.

*Daddy*

# BOB TEAGUE *to his son Adam*

*Bob Teague (1929– ) was the first African-American newsman hired by the NBC television network. In addition to newscaster, he has been a reporter for* The Milwaukee Journal *and* The New York Times, *and has written a number of books, including* The Flip Side of Soul: Letters to my Son *(1989), from which the following letter and the one on page 103 were taken. Adam is his only child.*

*Dear Wounded Survivor from a Broken Home:*
In another of my recurring daydreams of life in the promised land, I see marching regiments of black refugees from shattered families like ours. They are striving to recover, picking themselves up and getting back in the race to catch the 7:19 from Larchmont to success.

Furthermore, I see an eloquent extension of my persona persuading young dudes like you to pounce on any chance to go to college.

I have yet to confirm my theory that maybe your no-college-now stance was some sort of protest—or an expression of pain. Like the body blows you must have felt during the disintegration of our family. I shared that pain. Which perhaps explains the distraction that prevented me from communicating to you some of the unadvertised rewards of higher learning, regardless of whatever other goals one may pursue. When you were younger I focused too narrowly on the link between education and employment and the need to accumulate money as a shield against the worst improprieties of racism. I should have been selling the poetry, beauty, and magic that education brings to one's life and the way it stirs the soul. And the learning process continues, with escalating diversity, at higher speeds. In my experience, the relationships between things, events, ideas, and circumstances became less puzzling, more instructive. I began to recognize patterns, anomalies, mistakes, and triumphs of civilized folks over the centuries. I began to anticipate errors and disasters, then profit from my perceptions. More important, I began to experience the heady elation that comes with the effort to create ideas and works of art.

To make amends for my oversight, I yearn to find some supernatural technique to implant a little magic in the brains of disadvantaged children. I am talking about the kind of magic that would lift their aspirations well beyond their current popular desire to become rich and famous as members of yet another jiving bastard-rhyming rap group. At the same time, I want to see black parents working up raps of their own to steer their kids onto the right tracks. "Would you like to discuss some ways and means that might help you to stop flushing your life down the toilet?" Or, "As long as you are under this roof, you will obey the house rules."

Somehow I must sell the excitement of learning. I am thinking now about my freshman course in Zoology I at Wisconsin more than thirty-five years ago. It astonished me to see certain animals, untrained by man, using tools.

*better than Da! 1954! @ age 25!*

A predatory fish, hovering just below the surface of a river, spits water against the underside of leaves that overhang the water, the idea being to dislodge insects squatting topside. Once the little buggers hit the surface—gulp!

An African chimp pokes a skinny stick into an underground colony of living hors d'oeuvres; when he retracts the stick, it is crawling with delicious captives. Gulp!

A huge bird lays an egg so tough she has to pick up a marble-sized rock with her beak and fling it at the egg, again and again, to break the shell and hatch her little darling.

23

A clever otter carries a flat rock when he dives for oysters; upon returning to the surface with a closed oyster shell in his mouth, he floats on his back, balances the rock on his tummy, and slams the shellfish against it with both paws. Gulp!

Think for a moment, speculate. What different bright ideas might have eventually come to me and my classmates after becoming aware of such phenomena? Isn't it amazing what college professors—the Svengalis of civilization—can do with the magic of ideas? They fill young brains with the stuff that creates more room for thinking.

Maybe I should have hired a task force of Madison Avenue consultants to arouse lust in your heart for an alma mater. Or maybe I should have updated a family legend that defined the peer pressure that nudges adolescents into the mainstream. Long, long ago, your great-granddaddy told me when I was a boy, our tribal ancestors in Africa invented sort of a practical bar mitzvah for young blacks. To achieve manhood, around sixteen years of age each aspiring hunter-warrior faced a dangerous test. Alone, he had to trek into the bush, armed with only a spear, and kill a lion. Or die. Since the tribe could neither prosper nor survive without a steady supply of tough buck privates trained to hunt animals and fight men, every institution within the tribe herded the unsuspecting prospects into the prep school. That was the magic in their lives—the basis of their hopes for a long and happy tomorrow. To be on that track meant status. Not to be meant disgrace. Scarcely anyone dared to risk a lifetime of diminished respect from their friends and neighbors. Such a fate, the boys were taught from infancy, would truly be worse than death. So they willingly enrolled—dedicating themselves to acquiring discipline, skill, knowledge, courage, and stamina to earn their place in the tribe. And they stayed the course. Dropping out was unthinkable. Eventually, they were prepared to face whatever challenge might threaten their people.

If I'm lucky, I will find a way to translate that legend into the language of the nineties. Gradually, black families would develop the necessary auxiliary concepts and institutions to support the new legend: In order to become a respected and useful member of our tribe, young blacks must strive for and scheme for even the skinniest chance to reach college, because everybody knows that's where it's at.

# ON CLEANLINESS
## AND GROOMING

# LORD CHESTERFIELD *to his son Philip*

*The eighteenth century isn't known for its rigorous attitudes about personal hygiene. People rarely bathed; streets and stairwells doubled as lavatories. Nevertheless, Lord Chesterfield was almost obsessive in insisting that his son be clean and well groomed. In a 1749 letter he wrote: "A thorough cleanliness in your person is as necessary for your own health, as it is not to be offensive to other people."*

◆ ◆ ◆

*November 1750*

*Dear Boy,*

You will possibly think that this letter turns upon strange, little trifling objects; and you will think right, if you consider them separately; but if you take them aggregately, you will be convinced that, as parts, which conspire to form that whole, called the exterior of a man of fashion, they are of importance. I shall not dwell now upon those personal graces, that liberal air, and that engaging address, which I have so often recommended to you; but descend still lower—to your dress, cleanliness, and care of your person.

When you come to Paris, you must take care to be extremely well dressed, that is, as the fashionable people are. This does by no means consist in the finery, but in the taste, fitness, and manner of wearing your clothes; a fine suit ill-made, and slatternly or stiffly worn, far from adorning, only exposes the awkwardness of the wearer. Get the best French tailor to make your clothes, whatever they are, in the fashion, and to fit you, and then wear them; button them or unbutton them, as the genteelest people you see do. Let your man learn of the best *friseur* to do your hair well, for that is a very material part of your dress. Take care to have your stockings well gartered up, and your shoes well buckled; for nothing gives a more slovenly air to a man than ill-dressed legs.

In your person you must be accurately clean; and your teeth, hands, and nails should be superlatively so. A dirty mouth has real ill consequences to the owner, for it infallibly causes the decay, as well as the intolerable pain of the teeth; and it is very offensive to his acquaintance, for it will most inevitably stink. I insist therefore that you wash your teeth the first thing that you do every morning, with a soft sponge and warm water, for four or five minutes, and then wash your mouth five or six times. Mouton, whom I desire you will send for upon your arrival at Paris, will give you an opiate, and a liquor to be used sometimes. Nothing looks more ordinary, vulgar, and illiberal, than dirty hands, and ugly, uneven and ragged nails. I do not suspect you of that shocking, awkward trick of biting yours; but that is not enough; you must keep the ends of them smooth and clean—not tipped with black, as the ordinary people's always are. The ends of your nails should be small segments of circles, which, by a very little care in the cutting, they are very easily brought to; every time that you wipe your hands, rub the skin round your nails backwards, that it may not grow up and shorten your nails too much. The cleanliness of the rest of your person, which by the way will conduce greatly to your health, I refer from time to time to the bagnio. My mentioning these particulars arises (I freely own) from some suspicion that the hints are not unnecessary; for when you were a schoolboy, you were slovenly and dirty above your fellows. I must add another caution, which is, that upon no account whatever you put your fingers, as too many people are apt to do, in your nose or ears. It is the most shocking, nasty, vulgar rudeness that can be offered to company; it disgusts one, it turns one's stomach; and, for my own part, I would much rather [know] that a man's fingers were actually in his breech, than see them in his nose. Wash your ears well every morning, and blow your nose in your handkerchief whenever you have occasion; but, by the way, without looking at it afterwards.

# JACK LONDON *to his daughter Joan*

*Jack London (1876–1916), author of* The Call of the Wild, The Sea-Wolf, White Fang, *and numerous other best-selling adventure novels, married his first wife, Bessie, in 1900 and left her three years later, after falling in love with Charmian Kittredge. The divorce, a prolonged and hostile affair, wasn't made final until November 18, 1905; the next day London married Kittredge.*

*London once wrote to his publisher: "Right here at the start please know you are dealing with a man who is always hopelessly frank." And London was frank in almost all his correspondence, even—and possibly to a fault—that to his ex-wife and their two daughters, Joan and Bess. In a letter to the older, Joan, London asked: "What have you done for me in all the days of your life? What do you* feel *for me? Am I merely your meal-ticket? Do you look upon me as merely a creature with a* whim, *or* fancy, *or* fantasy, *that compels him to care for you and to take care of you?—because he is a fool who gives much and receives . . . well, receives nothing?" These are harsh words from anyone, but they are especially so coming from a thirty-seven-year-old to his daughter of only twelve.*

*The harshness can be explained in part by London's personal circumstances around that time, 1913: His ex-wife had forbidden his daughters to visit him on his California ranch. His new wife had lost one child two days after it was born and a second through miscarriage. His house was destroyed by fire, and he was operated on for appendicitis, only to be informed he suffered from a kidney disease. It would take his life three years later.*

◆ ◆ ◆

*Glen Ellen, California*
*September 16, 1915.*

*Dear Joan:*

First of all, I had Aunt Eliza send you the check for $7.00 so that you might buy the two pairs of boots for yourself and Bess.

Second of all, I promised to reply to your letter.

Third of all, and very important, please remember that your Daddy is a very busy man. When you write to society people, or to young people, who have plenty of time, write on your fine stationery and write on both sides of the paper. But, please, when you write to Daddy, take any kind of paper, the cheapest paper for that matter, and write on one side only. This makes it ever so much easier for Daddy to read. A two-sheet letter, such as yours that I am now looking at, written on both sides, is like a Chinese puzzle to a busy man. I take more time trying to find my way from one of the four portions into which your two-sided sheet is divided than I do in reading the letter itself.

Some day I should like to see you in your French heeled slippers. Joan, you are on the right track. Never hesitate at making yourself a dainty, delightful girl and woman. There is a girl's pride and a woman's pride in this, and it is indeed a fine pride. On the one hand, of course, never over-dress. On the other hand, never be a frump. No matter how wonderful are the thoughts that burn in your brain, always, physically, and in dress, make yourself a delight to all eyes that behold you.

I have met a number of philosophers. They were real philosophers. Their minds were wonderful minds. But they did not take baths, and they did not change their socks and it almost turned one's stomach to sit at table with them.

Our bodies are as glorious as our minds, and, just as one cannot maintain a high mind in a filthy body, by the same token one cannot keep a high mind and high pride in a fine body when said body is not dressed beautifully, delightfully, charmingly. Nothing would your Daddy ask better of you in this world than that you have a high mind, a high pride, a fine body, and, just as all the rest, a beautifully dressed body.

I do not think you will lose your head. I think, as I read this last letter of yours, that I understand that you have balance, and a woman's balance at that. Never forget the noble things of the spirit, on the other hand, never let your body be ignoble, never let the garmenture of your body be ignoble. As regards the garmenture of your body, learn to do much with little, never to over-do, and to keep such a balance between your garmenture and your mind that both garmenture and mind are beautiful.

I shall not say anything to you about your method of saving, about Bess's method of saving, but there is much I should like to say to you, and, in the meantime I think a lot about it. You are on the right track. Go ahead. Develop your mind to its utmost beauty; and keep your body in pace with your mind.

*[Daddy]*

# On Sportsmanship

# RUDYARD KIPLING *to his son John*

"Have you news of my boy Jack?"
*Not this tide.*
"When d'you think that he'll come back?"
*Not with this wind blowing, and this tide.*
—From "My Boy Jack"

*In her diary entry of August 15, 1915, Rudyard Kipling's wife, Carrie, wrote of their son's departure for war: "He looks very straight and smart and young, as he turns at the top of the stairs to say: 'Send my love to Daddo.'" Two days later John Kipling was in France—and six weeks after that he was dead, killed in the battle of Loos, a confrontation that cost the British twenty thousand lives and did not win the war as it was supposed to. The telegram the Kiplings received pronounced John missing in action; his body was never found.*

*For many years Kipling struggled with his son's death. He had encouraged John to enlist; he had glorified war in many of his stories and poems. In his writing, Kipling returned time and again to John's death—in such poems as "The Gardener," "My Boy Jack," and "The Children—1914–1918."*

*The letter that follows was written in 1909, two months before John's twelfth birthday; he was away at school.*

◆ ◆ ◆

*Bateman's,*
*Burwash,*
*Sussex.*
*June. 16. 1909.*

*Dear old man—*

I wasn't going to write to you this week on account of coming over on Saturday but seeing that your sports begin on Saturday I just want to breathe a few moral maxims in your ear "said Mr Campbell".

You are now getting on in life—like Elsie—and I want your behaviour to correspond with your years. Therefore, O my Son, do all that you can to win, honestly and fairly the events for which you have entered. If you win, shut your head. Exalt not yourself nor your legs nor your wind nor anything else that is yours. To boast (not that you are given to it) is the mark of the Savage and the Pig. If you lose remember that you have lost. It doesn't matter one little bit but it matters a great deal if you go about jawing about your handicap being too heavy or your having had a bad start or your being tripped or put off. The man who explains why he lost and hints that under other circumstances he might have won is worse than the Pig and the Savage. Remember that, *mon ami*. We shall be equally delighted whether you win or lose as long as you do both of them, as you always have hitherto, decently and quietly. Only *don't* join the knot of little shrimps who always exist in every school, who always jaw and jabber and explain if they happen to have lost an event.

Elsie has a H A T! I haven't letters big enough for the article, but it is a

I don't know whether she will come in it. She can't if there is any wind or any-one else on the cricket field. Our plan is to come into Brighton early on Sat. morning and do an hour at the dentist's. Then to Aunt G's for lunch and then directly to the sports. Tea with you in the school and then home. Hurroo!

Did I tell you—or did anyone tell you—we came home by the Wick the other day? We'll try it again on Saturday—*unberufen*. Great and joyous love from us all,

> *Ever your*
> *Pater.*

P.S. Caught 5 fish to-day in the pond. Mother caught 4—Col. Feilden 1. I lent my moral support. We are trying to catch the fish and then to poison the weed.

# ON TRAVEL

# JOHANN WOLFGANG VON GOETHE
*to his son August*

---

*In the summer of 1786, Johann Wolfgang von Goethe, then thirty-seven, left Weimar and traveled south, to Italy. The country, which he had wanted to visit since childhood, was everything he had hoped it would be, and he stayed there almost two years, most of the time in Rome, where he finished his play* Iphigenia in Tauris *and added scenes to* Faust. *Goethe's passion for Italy continued throughout his life, and he revisited it often in his writings, in such works as* Roman Elegies, Venetian Epigrams, *and of course* Italian Journey.

*Of his return to Weimar, Goethe wrote, "I had come back from Italy, so rich in forms, to shapeless Germany; I had to exchange a bright sky for a dull one."*

*More than four decades later Goethe's only son, August, made the same trip south—and for many of the same reasons. He was forty years old, restless and unhappy in Germany, and he hoped to cure himself by exchanging the dull northern skies for bright southern ones. But August did not survive the trip. He died in Rome—probably from smallpox—in October 1830, four months after his father wrote him the letter that follows. "It was surely a supreme touch of irony," J. G. Robertson observes in his biography of Goethe, "that [August] should have died in that Rome which had once been for his father the portal to a higher life, and be buried at the base of the pyramid of Cestius, which Goethe had once hoped would be his own final resting-place."*

*Goethe himself died in 1832. August's mother, Christiane Volpius, whom Goethe had married when their son was sixteen, had died in 1816.*

♦ ♦ ♦

*Weimar*
*June 29, 1830*

By the strangest chances it was only to-day that I read your little note, Milan the 2nd June. So that is why it is not mentioned in my letter of the 27th.

Nevertheless this is to tell you that I am preparing to send you something to Rome and presume that you will be going there. You will probably receive this letter and that one at the same time, and let me say most explicitly and solemnly that I will be very pleased indeed to read in your diary of your entry by the Porta del Popolo. Now that the journey has already done you so much good in mind and body, you should be able to decide with increasing ease and freedom what may be useful to you in the future.

According to your note you returned from Venice by way of Florence and Genoa to Milan; so I should say you could now go on to Rome either more quickly or by some other way. From this distance I can give you no advice at all on this. The main thing is still for you to come into contact with new objects and new people. So think over on your own and with our good friend Mylius what would be best. Go to places you have not yet seen, glean more from those you have seen; every place can then yield the greatest treasures.

On your tour to the South, whether you go by Lodi, Piacenza, Parma, Reggio, Bologna and Ravenna to the Adriatic, or whether you come from Rimini on that coast to [Loreto] and then on to Rome, is for you to decide and to carry out with the same good sense as before. You must always remind yourself that your aim is to absorb a great world and to free your mind of any cramping limitations. You must convince yourself that with this in view it is of no importance even if you miss a few agate-beads out of the much-praised rosary. So you can assure Mylius the banker in Milan in my name that I shall refund any and every sum made over to you and shall at once settle any bills of exchange.

You will hardly complete the journey you sketch out from Venice in four weeks, so this letter will probably reach you in Milan.

If, as is quite possible, Eckermann [Goethe's secretary] is now satisfied with what he has seen, give him the means to return in comfort; he shall be welcome here, with all that he has to bring. I am looking forward to seeing the medals; if you find others like them, do not grudge the outlay on them. We have of course some excellent ones already: but there are still many going about, recognized and unrecognized. Bertholdo's medal of Mahomet the Second, for instance, instructs and delights me every day. While you are looking 'round you in the wide world, I am once more enjoying some etchings and drawings acquired for moderate sums; the artist's spirit shines out in them even though his achievements have been greater. Herr von Mueller sends best greetings and is pleased at your praising the original of the Madonna in Venice, for he was delighted with even a copy in Bologna. Ottilie [August's wife] sends special greetings; she is not well, but dear and good as ever. Your little girl grows more amusing every day.

And so on and on.

# ON CAREER

# SHERWOOD ANDERSON *to his son John*

*Twice in his life Sherwood Anderson (1876–1941) traveled to Europe. During the first trip, in 1921, he met many important writers of his generation, James Joyce and Gertrude Stein among them. On his second trip, in December 1926, he was accompanied by Elizabeth Prall, the third of his four wives, and two of his three children from his first marriage: John, almost eighteen, and Marion, fifteen.*

*The letters to John below were written in the spring of 1927, after Anderson had returned to the United States; his son had remained in Europe to study painting. Anderson was closer to John than he was to either his daughter or his older son, Robert. He considered John a kindred spirit and, as these letters attest, wanted him to be an artist.*

◆ ◆ ◆

*[Troutdale, Virginia]*
*[April 1927]*

Something I should have said in my letter yesterday.

In relation to painting.

Don't be carried off your feet by anything because it is modern, the latest thing.

Go to the Louvre often and spend a good deal of time before the Rembrandts, the Delacroix's [*sic*].

Learn to draw. Try to make your hand so unconsciously adept that it will put down what you feel without your having to think of your hands.

Then you can think of the thing before you.

Draw things that have some meaning to you. An apple, what does it mean?

The object drawn doesn't matter so much. It's what you feel about it, what it means to you.

A masterpiece could be made of a dish of turnips.

Draw, draw, hundreds of drawing[s].

Try to remain humble. Smartness kills everything.

The object of art is not to make salable pictures. It is to save yourself.

Any cleanness I have in my own life is due to my feeling for words.

The fools who write articles about me think that one morning I suddenly decided to write and began to produce masterpieces.

There is no special trick about writing or painting either. I wrote constantly for 15 years before I produced anything with any solidity to it.

For days, weeks, and months now I can't do it.

You saw me in Paris this winter. I was in a dead, blank time. You have to live through such times all your life.

The thing, of course, is to make yourself alive. Most people remain all of their lives in a stupor.

The point of being an artist is that you may live.

Such things as you suggested in your letter the other day. I said, "Don't do what you would be ashamed to tell me about."

I was wrong.

You can't depend on me. Don't do what you would be ashamed of before a sheet of white paper or a canvas.

The materials have to take the place of God.

About color. Be careful. Go to nature all you can. Instead of paintshops, other men's palettes, look at the sides of buildings in every light. Learn to observe little thing[s], a red apple lying on a grey cloth.

Trees, trees against [a] hill, everything. I know little enough. It seems to me that if I wanted to learn about color, I would try always to make a separation. There is a plowed field here before me, below it a meadow, half-decayed cornstalk[s] in the meadow making yellow lines, stumps, some-times like looking into an ink bottle, sometimes almost blue.

The same in nature is a composition.

You look at it, thinking, "What made up that color?" I have walked over a piece of ground, after seeing it from a distance, trying to see what made the color I saw.

Light makes so much difference.

You won't arrive. It is an endless search.

I write as though you were a man. Well, you must know my heart is set on you.

It isn't your success I want. There is a possibility of your having a decent attitude toward people and work. That alone may make a man of you.

*Dear John:*

"Sunday morning and raining." I had just written the above sentence, intending to write you a long letter, when I put the sheet aside and began writing on my book. I have perhaps written [2,000] or 3,000 words since then. Now I am tired and my hands are shaky. It is still raining, harder than ever. I shall have to take a drink of moon to write to you at all.

What I want to say is something about the delight that may finally come to you in such moments of work. You may come to get out of canvases what I get out of sheets of paper.

I presume it is the power of losing self. Self is the grand disease. It is what we all are trying to lose.

I think the reason I want you to be an artist, have an artist's viewpoint, is just because such times compensate for so much else.

How people ever lose themselves who are not artists I do not know. Perhaps they, some of them, do it in love.

To love a woman and possess her is a good deal. It isn't enough for an eager man.

Power, such as comes with achievement, is something. In the end it becomes a disease. It destroys the man who has it.

In art there is the possibility of impersonal love. For modern men it is, I think, the only road to God.

I presume that is why, loving you as my son, I want you to be an artist. I don't really give a damn whether you succeed or not.

There is a lot to say, but I am too tired to write.

I will just send this broken fragment off to you.

# EUGENE O'NEILL *to his son Shane*

*O'Neill's relationships with his second son, Shane, and his daughter, Oona, were colored in part by his rancorous association with their mother, Agnes Boulton, whom he married in 1918 and divorced in 1929. (He married Carlotta Monterey, with whom he had been living for quite some time, three weeks after divorcing Agnes.)*

*Shane was twenty when his father—by then a Nobel Prize–winning playwright—wrote the following letter. Shane had had trouble since school and now was having difficulty choosing a career path: he wanted to study art; he wanted to go into the movies; he wanted to breed horses. Although O'Neill himself had been deeply troubled at his son's age, he was not particularly sympathetic to Shane's plight.*

*Sadly, Shane never managed to find his way: he drank heavily, took drugs, and was arrested for possession of heroin. He attempted suicide, like his father, and succeeded, like his older brother, in 1977.*

◆ ◆ ◆

*Tao House*
*Danville*
*Contra Costa County*
*California*
*July the 18th 1939*

*Dear Shane,*

I wrote Oona a couple of days ago to tell you to expect an answer to your letter soon and here it is.

My feeling, that Harry spoke to you about—and by the way, I didn't tell him to say anything to you—was based on the fact that you had let me hear so little from you at Lawrenceville. But forget it. I appreciate a lot the frankness of this last letter of yours and I hope you will always write me in just that spirit. What you say of your feeling a new understanding had sprung up between us on your last visit was exactly what I felt. Which made it doubly hard to comprehend why later on you went ahead with a complete change in your plans without consulting me and were all booked for Lawrenceville by the time I heard from you.

My advice on the subject of raising horses would not be much use to you. I don't know anyone in that game, what conditions or prospects are, or anything else about it. All I know is that if you want to get anywhere with it, or with anything else, you have got to adopt an entirely different attitude from the one you have had toward getting an education. In plain words, you've got to make up your mind to study whatever you undertake, and concentrate your mind on it, and really work at it. This isn't wisdom. Any damned fool in the world knows it's true, whether it's a question of raising horses or writing plays. You simply have to face the prospect of starting at the bottom and spending years learning how to do it. The trouble with you, I think, is that you are still too dependent on others. You expect too much from outside you and demand too little of yourself. You hope everything will be made smooth and easy for you by someone else. Well, it's coming to the point where you are old enough, and have been around enough, to see that this will get you exactly nowhere. You will be what you make yourself and you have got to do that job absolutely alone and on your own, whether you're in school or holding down a job.

After all, parents' advice is no damned good. You know that as well as I. The best I can do is to try to encourage you to work hard at something you really want to do and have the ability to do. Because any fool knows that to work hard at something you want to accomplish is the only way to be happy. But beyond that it is entirely up to you. You've got to do for yourself all the seeking and finding concerned with what you want to do. Anyone but yourself is useless to you there.

I'm glad you got the job on the party-fishing boat. It's a start in the right direction of independence. The more you get to know of independence the better you will like it, and the more you will get to know yourself and the right aim for your life.

What I am trying to get firmly planted in your mind is this: In the really important decisions of life, others cannot help you. No matter how much they would like to. You must rely only on yourself. That is the fate of each one of us. It can't be changed. It just is like that. And you are old enough to understand this now.

And that's all of that. It isn't much help in a practical advice way, but in another way it might be. At least, I hope so.

I'm glad to know of your doing so much reading and that you're becoming interested in Shakespeare. If you really like and understand his work, you will have something no one can ever take from you.

We are looking forward to Oona's visit. I appreciate your writing about her as you did. It is so long since I have seen her. Too long. Ordinarily I would have been coming East every year or two to put on new plays and would have seen her then. But a Cycle of nine plays is another matter. It brings up complications that keep me tied down to the job, especially as I have not yet caught up on my schedule from the delay my long illness of two years ago caused.

Don't talk of dry spell! We know all about that! We had hardly any rain last winter and now we live in dread our springs will get so low before the summer ends that a lot of the stuff we have planted around the house can't be watered and will have to die. It's rotten. Natives tell us there was less rain this year than at any time for forty years.

Carlotta joins me in love to you. Let me know as soon as you have any definite plans for the immediate future. And keep your chin up! You will be all right as soon as you get yourself organized along one set line.

*As ever, Father*

# HARRY TRUMAN *to his daughter Margaret*

*Mary Margaret Truman was the only child of President Harry Truman (1884–1972) and his wife, Bess. She was also the first daughter of a president of the United States to pursue her own career. Margaret wanted to be a singer. Her mother was against it but her father gave his support. In a letter to his mother and sister, Truman wrote of his daughter's plans: "If she wants to be a warbler and has the talent and will do the hard work necessary to accomplish her purpose, I don't suppose I should kick."*

*Margaret made her singing debut in Detroit, in 1947, a year after the following letter of encouragement was written. Truman's biographer David McCullough comments: "Possibly no vocal performer in history had ever appeared for the first time under such pressure, or before so big an audience and so many critics." Reviews of Margaret's first performance were kind, if lukewarm in their praise, but as she continued to sing, criticism grew harsh.*

*In 1950, she came to the nation's capital and performed to a sold-out audience of 3,500; among those in attendance were her father and Paul Hume, the music critic for* The Washington Post. *Hume's review the next morning was scathing. "Miss Truman," he felt, "cannot sing very well. She is flat a good deal of the time. . . . There are few moments during her recital when one can relax and feel confident that she will make her goal, which is the end of the song."*

*Truman's defense of his daughter was extreme in its vituperation, and when it ran, on page one of the* News, *it embarrassed the White House and the presidency. The president wrote that he had "just read [Hume's] lousy review of Margaret's concert"; he accused Hume of being "a frustrated old man who wishes he could have been successful," said he was "off the beam," and promised that if the two of them should ever meet, Hume would "need a new nose, a lot of beefsteak for black eyes, and perhaps a supporter below!"*

*To a nation whose children were dying in the Korean War, the president's almost rabid defense of his daughter's singing career was seen as inappropriate. Letters flooded in, expressing shock and outrage. "Our boys died," one writer said, "while your infantile mind was on your daughter's review." Another observed: "One major regret at this time is that your daughter was not there to receive the same treatment as our son received in Korea."*

◆ ◆ ◆

*Sunday, December 21, 1946*

*Dear Margie:—*

You don't know how much your old daddy appreciated your good letter. Glad you had the chance to sleep in a lower for once. Did Vietta sleep in the upper? I've been wondering where she slept. You must have had a grand trip from St. Louis with the snooty and talkative Mrs. Sonter. When we were kids she and her sister and George never felt that your pop was good enough to associate with the children of a college president—even if the college was in a fading condition. But I never cared. She had a black sheep brother named Paul who was a regular guy and who always had a good time with us roughnecks of the lower strata. Your ma was upper crust too but she wasn't snooty like the Bryants. You understand you don't know anything about this. Because since those days your pa never pretends he remembers and he's done favors and was glad to for all of them including the lowbrow black sheep.

Now I heard you say the other evening when we were discussing your career that you were after the big money. Now that I don't approve of. I want you to have artistic perfection—and the money will come of itself. I want you to be a truly great singer and not Kate Smith or a radio crooner. When you have attained artistic perfection all the rest will come. Service then to the pleasure of people will make you great. And I mean service to the higher instincts of the people. There are lowbrows who'll never appreciate the good you do who make burlesque singers a success. I don't want you to

be burlesque—I want you to be the real thing and I am sure, now, that you can.

So take it in stride and do it right. It is the hard way but the best way. When your pa ran for the Eastern Judge the wise old boys told me you can never do any good in that office. I did though because I gave service to the people. I didn't want to be Presiding Judge. I had to take it. I didn't want to be Senator—it was forced upon me and you know the rest. I worked at each job to put the best in me into it for service—and look at my most terrible windup. Maybe I shouldn't have mentioned it.

Kiss mamy for me + tell your grandmas your aunts, uncles and cousins hello.

*XXXXXXXX Dad*
*OOOO*

# JOHN CHEEVER *to his son Fred*

*Short story writer and novelist John Cheever (1912–1982) was, in his own words, "the father of three comely and brilliant children": a daughter, Susan, and two sons, Benjamin and Federico (Fred). In his introduction to his father's letters, Benjamin Cheever writes: "You take the people you love pretty much the way you find them. Their worst qualities are often linked with their very best ones." As his children found him, John Cheever was a "man of massive and fundamental contradictions. . . . Despite, or perhaps because of these contradictions, [he] was successful, not just as a writer of fiction but as a father, a husband, friend and lover. And he was great fun."*

*Nothing testifies to Cheever's greatness as a father—or his fun—as well as his letters. The good humor and trenchant optimism of the following one, written to his younger son, are particularly poignant when one considers that Cheever was ill with cancer when he wrote it. A father at the end of his life and career speaks of his son's "own brilliant destiny," a destiny the father knows he will not live to witness. The letter was written some two months before the elder Cheever died.*

◆ ◆ ◆

*April 17th, 1982*

Dear Fred,

To search out a career through finding a group of sympathetic colleagues seems to me madness. The tradition of the guilds (and the Italian schools) ended with the sixteenth century when the recognition of individual talent ended the middle ages. To seek sympathetic colleagues is rather like seeking a guild. You have your own brilliant destiny and as you develop your accomplishments you will, with luck, find yourself in the company of men and women who are similarly accomplished. Can you think of a distinguished man in any field who chose his profession because of the splendor of his colleagues. This is not fatherly advice. The only fatherly advice I have ever given you is not to eat your peas off a knife.

On librarians I do speak with predjudice [*sic*]. The profession in general has always seemed to me like the legitimization and financing of an impulse to collect old socks. It has always seemed to enjoy people who would enjoy handling old socks, smelling old socks and legislating categories of old socks. But then you know I am terribly predjudiced.

Since the first announcement of Susie's pregnancy the growth and arrival of little Sarah has seem [*sic*] to be the most natural sort of growth and today they take the baby home. Tad is quite as involved in the naturalness as Susie and they both seem to me to be quite lovely people.

Ben and Janet had just left for Boston to run in the marathon. My love to Mary.

*Yours,*
*John*

# ON MILITARY SERVICE

# DANIEL WEBSTER *to his son Fletcher*

*Daniel Webster (1782–1852) had five children, only one of whom, Fletcher, survived him. A son and a daughter died in childhood; another son and daughter, Edward and Julia, died in 1848 (Edward in the Mexican War, and Julia of tuberculosis).*

*Webster was a stern father. In 1837 he wrote to Edward, who was away at school:*

*I return your letter, in which you will find as many errors, as you see marks.*

*There are mispellings;*

*There is no tolerably correct punctuation;*

*There are instances, in which sentences, after periods, are begun with small letters; and words, which should be begun with large letters, are begun with small ones.*

*Write me, immediately, a more careful, & a better, letter—*

*When his father wrote him, Fletcher Webster was twenty-two and on an expedition to the Midwest to purchase land.*

*[January 15, 1836]*

I am sorry for your disappointment about the aid-ship; but never mind, I believe you are as well without it; if you think not, I will see more about it, when I get home. I believe the military honors of our family terminated with my father. I once tried to be captain, and failed; and I canvassed a whole regiment to make your uncle an adjutant, and failed also. We are predestinated not to be great in the field of battle. We are not the sons of "Bellona's bridegroom"; our battles are forensic; we draw no blood, but the blood of our clients.

If, on a given occasion, a man can, gracefully, and without the air of a pedant, show a little more knowledge than the occasion requires, the world will give him credit for eminent attainments. It is an honest quackery. I have practised it, and sometimes with success.

We find connections and coincidences, helps and succors, where we did not expect them. I have never learned any thing which I wish to forget; except how badly some people have behaved; and I every day find, on almost every subject, that I wish I had more knowledge than I possess, seeing that I could produce it, if not for use, yet for effect.

# JOHN STEINBECK *to his son John*

---

*"When you have finished using a weapon," John Steinbeck (1902–1968) wrote to Lyndon Johnson in March 1965, "someone is dead or injured, but the product of the word can be life and hope and survival." It may seem surprising that the man who wrote this was, just a year later, defending the president's escalations in Vietnam. In May 1966, with his younger son preparing to go to war, Steinbeck wrote to Johnson again; he compared antiwar protesters to Tories and Copperheads and called their raised voices "the shrill squeaking of people who simply do not wish to be disturbed." His son John IV, he said, was "proud of his uniform and proud of his country."*

*It wasn't until the elder Steinbeck saw Vietnam for himself that he changed his mind. He traveled there in 1967 as a correspondent for* Newsday *and wrote home to friends: "Every dead G.I. . . . breaks your heart in a way that can never be repaired. If I could shorten this war by one hour by staying here, I would never come home."*

*Steinbeck's son also wrote about Vietnam, in the book* In Touch, *which was based on letters he sent to his father. "'Steinbeck,'" John IV writes in the book's introduction, "was the name stitched on my Army uniform, and I do not think it helped or hurt my ability to be drafted and sent to Vietnam like any other soldier."*

◆ ◆ ◆

*Sag Harbor [New York]*
*July 16, 1966*

Dear John:

I do know what you mean. I remember the same feeling when there were areas of trouble. "What the hell am I doing here? Nobody made me come." On the other hand, when it was over, I was usually glad I had gone. And one other thing. Once it started the blind panic went away and another dimension took its place. Thinking about it afterward I became convinced that there is some kind of built-in anaesthesia that balances and sets the terror back. Another thing that helps is the fact that you aren't alone. And everybody feels just as lousy when it is about to be. I don't know whether or not you took the Sneaky with you—that little leather flask. Fill it with whiskey—brandy is better. And it can be a great comfort to you. There's no law against false courage. It's better than none at all.

Now, let me discuss what you call your compulsion to be miserable. You think you had a choice—that you could just as well be in [San Francisco] with all the amenities, comfort, ease and a certain immunity from gunfire. Well, the fact of the matter with you as well as with me is that there wasn't really any choice. You did and will do what you are. If you had forced yourself to make the opposite choice you would have been in violation of yourself, and I truly believe you would have been much more miserable than you are. Of course I am worried about you, just terribly worried, but I am proud too that you have not violated what you are.

Also check with yourself on this. I know it was true of me. I had deep down convictions that I was a coward. I think everyone has. If I had broken or gone to pieces, I wouldn't have been surprised. But when it came and I didn't go haywire, when I was scared but no more scared than those around me, the sense of relief was like a flood of compensation. Because I think a good part of this particular fear is a fear of how you will behave. And no one knows for sure, until he has gone through it.

I was horrified when you asked me to get you orders to go out, but I couldn't have failed you there. Do you know, that is the only request I have ever made of the President? The only one. And I was not happy about making it. But if I had had to request that you *not* be sent, I think I would have been far more unhappy.

Please keep in touch. I love you.

Fa

# ON GOD AND RELIGION

# COTTON MATHER  *to his son Increase*

*Increase was the oldest of Cotton Mather's (1663–1728) fifteen children; he was also the greatest disappointment to his father.*

*The son did not go to Harvard; the father had been admitted to the university at age eleven and the grandfather (also Increase) had been the college president.*

*The father was a famous writer and pastor, a leader of New England Puritanism; the son went into debt, and was even accused of fathering a child with a prostitute.*

*Beyond the exhortations and Mather's fear for his son's soul, one hears in this letter a father's great disappointment—if not bewilderment—at his oldest son's refusal to follow in his footsteps.*

◆ ◆ ◆

*[c. August 1715]*

*Child,*

Solicitous I am that you may return unto me as fast as you can, and come into new methods as soon as [you] may, to qualify you for usefulness in the world.

But much more solicitous that you may return unto God and be withheld from sinning against Him.

A thing, for which it is impossible for me to express the pain of mind wherein you have long held me distressed.

You know not the child upon earth which has been more prayed for, and more talked to, that he might be converted unto God. And unto all the former means for your good there have now been added the admonitions of a pious uncle.

God forbid that you should be so infinitely unhappy as you must be if all these be lost upon you.

I hope you let not a day pass you without prayers to the glorious God. And that all the vices of dishonesty, debauchery, and false-speaking are abominable to you.

# JOHN JAMES RUSKIN *to his son John*

*"Surely the whole or the greatest part of the best men in Scripture were eminently men of the world," John James Ruskin comments to his only son in the letter below. And Ruskin (1785–1864) was himself a man of the world. The son of a grocer, he became a prosperous London wine merchant, a founding partner of Ruskin, Telford, and Domecq. His son, on the other hand, would be a man of words: the English art and literary critic and social reformer John Ruskin (1819–1900).*

*The younger Ruskin was twenty-two and a student at Oxford when his father wrote this letter, advising that "Heavenly subjects . . . be approached in the most worldly way." Ruskin graduated in 1842 and a year later published the first volume of* Modern Painters, *which secured his fame at the age of twenty-four. He went on to write four more volumes of* Modern Painters *(three of them under his parents' roof),* The Seven Lamps of Architecture, *the three-volume* Stones of Venice, *and numerous lectures and essays on social reform, among other works.*

*Despite his literary successes, John Ruskin's personal life was unhappy. After his marriage was annulled on the grounds that it had never been consummated, he returned to his parents' house. In 1858, now approaching forty, Ruskin fell in love with a nine-year-old girl, and when she later spurned him his health began to collapse.*

*Ruskin's father seems to have recognized early his son's precarious footing in the practical world, as the following suggests.*

◆ ◆ ◆

*London 25 Augt 1841.*

My dearest John

I have been looking at your Sunday Letter to Mama & leaving her & you to go into the Divinity of which I know nothing. I will but set down a few words. I think you are entirely right in the importance you attach to aiding others in their Difficulties & present *apparent* Lost state, but I would Say— after all that is said of middle Measures of halting between God & Mammon—that formed as we are half Body & half Spirit our Safety & our necessity is in the middle part. It hath ever appeared to me that we should seek the Light, but not approach it till we are blasted with Excess of Light. We should be zealous & approach the Heat of the Sun of Righteousness until we are warmed, but such is Human nature—if we approach it too nearly, we are Scorched Withered, Blasted. Human Reason is shattered into fragments & utter Ruin. It sounds paradoxical but these Heavenly subjects require to be approached in the most worldly way. We must hold to the anchor of Rationality, stick to our Humanities. We have Scripture warrant for this for surely the whole or the greatest part of the best men in Scripture were eminently men of the world, & even our Saviour himself. Was not one of the heaviest charges against him, that he associated with publicans & sinners—not for conversion only but for Fellowship.

I believe it safer for poor weak Creatures like ourselves, to walk in the track of Men distinguished by their *half*-worldly but wholly charitable conduct than to aim at some as yet unattempted flight. Our understanding & our feelings are too weak to sustain the Load you would impose upon them. No man could live under the daily & Nightly fear of Hell fire—As it is wisely ordered that all men think all men mortal but themselves so do the Dwellers upon Earth now—trust that they may be of the few who are to be Saved. Their belief is not strong but they have no ground to despair if we compare this with other ages of the world—but again it is an awful ground or rather a quick-*sand* of consolation that because compared with this age, so many people of former ages deserve to be d——d—your chance is the greater, admitting very few are to be saved. I am convinced however that many remain at ease from such vague undefined unconfessed feelings. But then comes the question—are you, or is any Individual capable of redeeming them or even of judging them so far as to attempt it. It rather jars upon my notions, & partakes of a presumption that any one doing all you lay down as necessary— would be intruding on the province of a God.

I am for great trust in the influence of the unaided Spirit for Salvation, but for all the assistance & devotion of our nature towards our fellowmen in their necessities. It seems to me that the voice of Heaven so calls us—That too much enthusiasm in Religion ends in Selfishness or Madness. There is safety in the walk of a St Carlo Borromeo. There is madness & selfishness only in that of a man who seeks to reach Heaven or draw others after him by coiling his Body up like a Rope & depositing himself in a cave three feet by two.

I never wish nor hope to find you a better preacher than St Paul yet who was more subject to the flesh. I say however I leave the Divinity to you & mama—

> *I am my dearest John*
> *Yr most affect*
> *Father*
> *JJR*

# NEAL CASSADY *to his daughter Cathleen*

*The year is 1958, the place San Francisco. "There has been," as Allen Ginsberg describes, "great exaltation, despair, prophecy, strain, suicide, secrecy, and public gaiety among the poets of the city." America is, in short, "having a nervous breakdown." The Beats, battling against the forces of mechanization and materialism, are taking the country by storm.*

*There are those among them who use "certain benevolent drugs." One is Neal Cassady (1926–1968). After giving three marijuana cigarettes to two men who have driven him home from a party, he is arrested, held, released—then arrested again. He is tried, found guilty, and sentenced to two terms of five years to life in prison for selling drugs.*

*During what turned out to be a two-year incarceration—first in the San Bruno county jail and later in San Quentin—Neal Cassady wrote many letters to his wife, Carolyn, and his three young children, Cathleen, Jamie, and John. As Carolyn explains in her introduction to* Grace Beats Karma, *the letters record Cassady's attempts, through religion, "to block thoughts of his unjust predicament and prevent the arousal of the fire-breathing dragon of rage coiled within, whose release would destroy him."*

*His words of advice to Cathleen on the occasion of her tenth birthday sound as though they were written more for himself than for her.*

*[September 5, 1958]*

*Dear Darling Daughter Cathleen JoAnne;*

Well, well, so at last my once wonderful little doll baby has grown into an even more wonderful big young lady. How does it feel to be almost five feet from tip to toe? Ten years ago you measured only 17½ inches. I know how tall you are getting by the fine picture of you on page 14 of the Saratoga News June 12th issue. It was taken when you were giving the proper three fingered salute and shaking the hand of Mrs. Gatewood while dressed in your attractive Brownie uniform. Yes, my lovely child, I'm most thrilled and proud to realize that you have completed your first decade (do you know what the word "decade" means and from what language it came?) and can finally, for the rest of your life in fact, right?, write your age down in double figures. So it is with real pleasure I send you my strongest wish for a very very happy birthday anniversary. Of course it's not your birthday but the day on which your nativity (what does the word "nativity" mean, can you guess?) is celebrated and so it's your anniversary, for example, the anniversary of our country's birthday is in July; can you tell me the exact day? By the way, if you are lucky enough to have a cake please, to help make you an even sweeter Cathy, (ha, ha, get the joke? its called a pun, meaning either a double play on words or playing on words with double, or more, meaning) eat a *small* piece just for me, will you? Naturally I'll write to you again yet, before I sign off for this time, dear offspring (know that word "offspring"?) I want to take this opportunity to remind you that God has favored you very much because there is hardly one girl in a million (thats a thousand times a thousand, isn't it?) who gets to be the big sister and only one in a billion (a thousand times a million, right?) who is allowed to take care of the family whenever their Mom or Dad is away. In other words He, God, is seeing to it that you get some good early practice in household duties and though you might feel at times like complaining (don't forget even the best of us do occasionally but, and heres the important point, we *try not* to since God forbids it) or wonder why you, being the child that's eldest, (I'll bet you know eldest means oldest, don't you?) were chosen to fill the most responsible post, you should never question your position, for its a greatly important one, but instead, especially whenever you are troubled by something you consider unfair, concentrate your budding awareness on remembering that *everything* that happens, good or bad, is all part of God's way to teach us His Holy plan. Personally, I believe He (always use capital letters when writing God, as I just did with His pronoun "He"—ask Mommy what a pronoun is) intends you to have several nice children of your own and is giving you this chance to learn (all life is just a school for us) to become more of a good mother-like person now so that it will be easier for you later on. Anyway, whether you have a large or small family in the future, you must begin spending an increased amount of time trying to overcome your dislikes by surrendering (giving up) your will (whatever you selfishly want that hurts others) to Jesus, as He has instructed *everyone* to do. Now this is very hard to accomplish successfully (do right) so hard, in fact, that it's the main problem of not only you, smart and pretty daughter, but of the whole world for most people, including, I'm afraid, part of your silly old daddy, finds it far too easy to be led into mistaken actions by chasing their unwise desires, nonetheless He, (God) who knows & forgives all this folly better than any 10 yr. old or anyone else on earth can imagine, still says He will reward only those who follow Him by doing the difficult tasks asked of them without giving in to either anger or carelessness. Therefore, to properly wear the crown of glory Jesus has waiting, you have to correctly perform (do right) the various things mother tells you, hard as they sometimes seem. Although its necessary to listen to your conscience and always let it be your guide, at your tender age you may not quite understand its dictates. So just remember, above all, that in proportion to how well you do the work you dislike most is how well you are making yourself lovely & pleasing to Jesus. After all, Cathy my love, He's right there in your very own heart so whenever you are in doubt about the right or wrong thing to do think of Him by closing your eyes and being real still until presently, if you stay *very* quiet, a warm feeling will creep over you and presto! the right way will pop into your mind. P.S. Tell Jamie & John that their letter will arrive tomorrow.

*Love, from your devoted Dad. N.*

# On Sex, Love, and Marriage

# LEO TOLSTOY *to his sons Ilya and Lev*

*Apart from his immense literary output, which included the novels* War and Peace *and* Anna Karenina, *Count Lev Nikolayevich Tolstoy (1828–1910) was the father of thirteen children. The letters that follow are to his third child, Ilya, and his fourth, Lev, respectively. Of the young Ilya, Tolstoy wrote in a letter to his wife: "Everything forbidden has its attraction for him, and he gets to know about it at once. . . . Ilya will come to grief unless he has a strict supervisor and one he loves." In the same letter, he described Lev as "good-looking, clever, a good memory, graceful. . . . I don't understand him properly yet."*

*Both sons married the women mentioned here. Like their father, both became writers. And both emigrated from Russia: Ilya went to the United States, where he died in 1933; Lev spent periods living in the United States, Italy, France, and Sweden, where he died in 1945.*

*Tolstoy's advice, his ambivalence toward the institution of marriage, was colored by personal experience. His relations with his wife, Sofya, whom he married in 1862, were rocky. By 1887, when he wrote to Ilya, his marriage had been in decline for years; he already had attempted to leave Sofya once, in 1884. But the marriage dragged on for another quarter-century, when, at the age of eighty-two, Tolstoy left home for good. He died in a train station, "a desperate old man," as Isaiah Berlin wrote, "beyond human aid, wandering self-blinded at Colonus."*

*Yasnaya Polyana*
*October 1887*

We got your letter to Tanya [one of Tolstoy's daughters], my dear Ilya, and I see you are still going ahead in the direction of the goal which is your objective, and I wanted to write to you and to her (because you probably tell her everything) to say what I think about it. I think about it a lot, with joy and fear alike.

This is what I think: To marry in order to enjoy oneself more will never work. To put marriage—union with the person you love—as your main aim, replacing everything else, is a big mistake. And it's obvious if you think about it. The aim is marriage. Well, you get married, and then what? If you have no other aim in life before marriage, then later on it will be terribly difficult, almost impossible for the two of you, to find one. It's almost certain that if you have no common aim before marriage, nothing will bring you together afterwards, and you will always be falling out. Marriage only brings happiness when there is a single aim—people meet on the road and say, 'Let's walk on together'; 'Yes, let's'; and offer one another their hands—and not when people are attracted to one another and then both turn off the road in different directions. In the first case it will be like this:

In the second, like this:

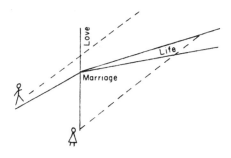

I say all this because the idea many people have that life is a vale of tears is just as false as the idea which the great majority have, and to which youth, health, and wealth incline you, that life is a place of entertainment. Life is a place of service, where one sometimes has occasion to put up with a lot that is hard, but more often to experience a great many joys. Only there can only be real joys when people themselves understand their life as service: have a definite aim in life outside themselves and their own personal happiness. Usually married people forget this completely. Marriage and the birth of children offer so many joyful things to look forward to that it seems that these things actually constitute life itself, but this is a dangerous delusion. If parents live and produce children without having any aim in life, they only put off the question of the aim of life and the punishment to which people are subjected when they live without knowing why—they only put it off, but they can't avoid it, because they will have to bring up and guide children and there will be nothing to guide them by. And then parents lose their human qualities and the happiness linked with them, and become pedigree cattle. So I say: People intending to marry because their life *seems* to them to be full, need more than ever to think and make clear to themselves what each of them is living for. And in order to make this clear, it's necessary to think, and to think hard about the conditions you live in and about your past, to estimate what you consider to be important and unimportant in life and to find out what you believe in—i.e., what you consider the invariable, indisputable truth, and what you will be guided by in life. And not only find out and make clear to yourself, but experience in practice and put into operation in your own life, because until you do what you believe in, you don't know whether you believe it or not. I know what you believe, and that belief, or those sides of it which are expressed in your actions, you need now more than at any other time to make clear to yourself by putting it into operation. Your belief is that good consists of loving people and being loved by them. To attain this, I know three activities which I constantly practice, which cannot be practiced often enough, and which are particularly necessary to you just now. The first—in order to be able to love people and be loved by them it is necessary to train oneself to require as little as possible from them, because if I require a lot and am deprived of many things, I'm inclined not to love but to reproach—this involves a lot of work. The second—in order to love people, not by word but by deed, it is necessary to teach oneself to do something useful for them. This involves even more work, especially for you at your age when it's natural for a person to be studying. The third—in order to love people and be loved by them, it is necessary to learn gentleness, humility, and the art of enduring unpleasant people and unpleasant things, and if it's impossible not to offend somebody, to be able to choose the least offense. And this involves the most work of all, and work which is non-stop, from waking up to going to sleep. And it's the most joyful sort of work, because day after day you can rejoice at your progress in it, and apart from that you gain the reward—insignificant at first but very joyful—of people's love.

And so I advise you, both of you, to think and to live as lovingly as possible, because only in this way will you find out whether you are really going along the same road and whether or not it's good for you to give one another your hands; and then if you are sincere, you will make your own future. Your aim in life should not be the joy of marriage, but that of bringing more love and truth into the world through your life. Then after that—marriage, in order to help one another to attain this aim.

*Les extrêmes se touchent*. The most egotistical and nasty life is the life of two people united in order to enjoy life, and the highest vocation is that of people who live in order to serve God by bringing good into the world, and uniting with each other for that purpose. Don't be confused—one is right and one is wrong. Why should man not choose what is higher? But once having chosen what is higher, it's necessary to put all one's heart and soul into it, not just a little bit of oneself; a little bit is no use. Well, I'm tired of writing, though there's more I wanted to say. I kiss you.

*Moscow*

*April 5, 1896*

I've been waiting for a letter from you, dear Lyova, in answer to mine, but then I decided to write to you without waiting, and now I've received your good letter. I'm very pleased about your marriage. I've no definite grounds for this, just a general feeling which makes me happier, and pleased that it's actually Dora Westerlund you will be marrying. Everything I know about her pleases me—the fact that she is Swedish, the fact that she is young, and especially the fact that you are very much in love with one another. As I wrote to you, I can't help being of the opinion, as [St.] Paul said, that it's better not to marry if you can, in order to serve God with all your strength. But if you can't, you should marry and hand on what you haven't finished yourself to the children you bring into the world. And if you marry, you should only marry when you simply can't help marrying. From all I can see, this is the case with you and Dora, and it's good when people are attracted to one another by the irresistible force of their whole being.

I'm an old man and you are young, and I would like to give you advice at such an important time of life. But it's difficult to give advice when people are far apart from each other in outlook. Intellectually I know you agree, and want to agree with me, but with your whole being you are remote, and she, because of her age, is still more remote. And so I would like to give the sort of advice where this difference won't be felt, and in which there won't be any demands which seem difficult. I have such advice, and I would like to give it to you in spite of the fact that it will probably be contrary to the advice given you by practical (that is, very unpractical) people. My advice is for you both to fetter your freedom as little as possible, not to undertake anything, not to make promises, not to arrange a definite form of life for yourselves but to *garder ses coudes franches*. You are so young that you still need to find out what you are, who you are, and what you are capable of, and therefore to learn in every way possible, to try to explain life to yourselves and to learn to live better without thinking of a form of life. This form will take shape of its own accord. Shake hands with your dear father-in-law-to-be and his wife and kiss Dora from me.

I'm well, although I feel I have aged. I'm still working happily on the statement of my beliefs. I make excursions into other works, but this is the main one. I devote my best powers to it.

Good-bye. I kiss you.

*L. T.*

*The father of psychoanalysis had six children, three daughters and three sons. Mathilde, born in 1887, was the oldest. As a child, she suffered from several serious illnesses: diphtheria nearly killed her in 1893, and in 1905 she almost died again— this time from internal bleeding after a botched appendicitis operation (her conditions left her unable to conceive). A series of smaller operations followed to remove cysts resulting from the first surgery.*

*In March 1908, she was in Meran, Austria (now Merano, Italy), recuperating from such an operation. In this letter, Freud's reassurances about his daughter's marriageability were prophetic and unnecessary. While in Meran, Mathilde met her future husband, a Viennese named Robert Hollitscher; she was married to him within a year.*

◆ ◆ ◆

*Vienna IX, Berggasse 19*
*March 19, 1908*

*My dear Mathilde*

It is the first time that you have asked me for help and you don't make it difficult for me this time, for it is easy to see that you are very much overrating your trouble and that you are drawing conclusions which according to my knowledge and information are quite out of place. I am not going to offer you any illusions, neither now nor at any other time; I consider them harmful and I know that the suspicion that they are illusions is enough to spoil the pleasure in them. But none is needed, anyhow. Meran is intended to strengthen you physically, for which it is very suitable; of course it cannot cure the local complaint; this has to take care of itself for the time being. It will probably go on giving you pain for several months (as a matter of fact your last attack sounds as though it may have been caused by a floating kidney), but it is harmless in itself; it is bound to shrink more and more and finally leave you altogether. Women often contract such things after childbirth, and they disappear without causing any trouble in later life. By the time the question of marriage arises in your life, you will be completely free of it. You know that I have always intended to keep you at home until you are at least twenty-four, until you are strong enough for the duties of marriage and possibly of bearing children, and until the weakness, which those three serious illnesses in your early life left behind, have been repaired. In social and material circumstances like ours, girls quite rightly do not marry during their early youth; otherwise their married life would be over too soon. You know that your mother was twenty-five when she married.

I think you probably associate the present minor complaint with an old worry about which I should very much like to talk to you for once. I have guessed for a long time that in spite of all your common sense you fret because you think you are not good-looking enough and therefore might not attract a man. I have watched this with a smile, first of all because you seem quite attractive enough to me, and secondly because I know that in reality it is no longer physical beauty which decides the fate of a girl, but the impression of her whole personality. Your mirror will inform you that there is nothing common or repellent in your features, and your memory will confirm the fact that you have managed to inspire respect and sympathy in any circle of human beings. And as a result I have felt perfectly reassured about your future so far as it depends on you, and you have every reason to feel the same. That you are my daughter shouldn't do you any harm, either. I know that finding a respected name and a warm atmosphere in her home was decisive in my choice of a wife, and there are certain to be others who think as I did when I was young.

The more intelligent among young men are sure to know what to look for in a wife—gentleness, cheerfulness, and the talent to make their life easier and more beautiful. I would be terribly sorry if your despondency were to make you change your direction, but let us hope that it is only a passing phase in a situation which many things have combined to produce. You have inherited your physical disposition from two of your aunts, both of whom you resemble more than your mother. I would rather you took after Aunt Minna than Aunt Rosa.

You have, my poor child, seen death break into the family for the first time, or heard about it, and perhaps shuddered at the idea that for none of us can life be made any safer. This is something all we old people know, which is why life for us has such a special value. We refuse to allow the inevitable end to interfere with our happy activities. So you, who are still so young, may as well confess that you really have no reason to be downhearted. I am very pleased to hear that the sun in Meran is doing you good. We would have pulled a very long face if you had returned as you left. You had better stay on as long as the Raabs are there and are willing to put up with you, let us hope until well into the month of May.

I greet you warmly and hope to hear from you again soon.

*Your loving*
*Father*

# GROUCHO MARX *to his daughter Miriam*

*In her introduction to* Love, Groucho, *Miriam Marx Allen writes: "My father was a great deal of joy and fun, as well as a stern parent. . . . There is one complaint I could make: quite possibly Groucho made himself too important in my life. He was so interesting and humorous that he made the boys and men I dated seem dull by comparison."*

*Groucho Marx had two other children besides Miriam, a son, Arthur, and a daughter, Melinda.*

◆ ◆ ◆

*February 28, 1947*

*Dear Mir:*

Finally got a letter from you and I hope you have completely recovered from your flu attack. I will be glad to pay your doctor bill, particularly if it aids you in recovering.

It is extremely gratifying to me to learn that you are now keeping company with four different men. I can understand your going around with Stanley, Al and John. John you say you met in an elevator. Was the elevator going up at the time, or down? This is very important, for going down in an elevator one always has that sinking feeling and for all I know you may have this confused with love. If you were going up, it is clearly a case of love at first sight and it also proves that he is a rising young man. I am a little baffled as to why you see David. A fat young anthropologist, probably covered with germs, doesn't sound like a very attractive suitor. Perhaps what your doctor diagnosed as intestinal flu was too close contact with David. As for the Japanese, I frankly don't know how I would feel having an enemy as a son-in-law.

Of course I realize that most sons-in-law are enemies anyway, but this could be an extremely sensitive relationship. We may be having dinner together some night and I might accidentally bring up the subject of Pearl Harbor and in the confusion all of the sukiyaki would fall on the carpet. At that, it would be a relief to meet someone older than me. At the moment practically everyone I know is thirty or forty years my junior and at times it makes me feel quite ancient.

We are planning on leaving here on the tenth and arriving in New York by train, weather and engineer permitting, on the thirteenth. As yet, however, we have no sleeping accommodations. I have suggested flying to Kay, but she resolutely declines to go up in the air. In fact she goes up in the air when I mention it. We may have to walk. However I will wire you before arriving.

You say you are going to quit your job on the seventeenth. I should arrive in New York on the thirteenth and I would like you to quit then so that we can spend some time together. If you then have to return to school before I return here, you will just have to make the trip weekly, with me, of course, defraying the expenses. Don't worry about that part of it. I miss you very much and I am very anxious to see you.

We previewed the picture for the second and last time last Tuesday in Pasadena with a house full of typical Pasadenians. You know, that young hoodlum crowd that screams hysterically when Andy Russell, or anyone like him, makes his appearance. They seemed very well satisfied with the picture, that is the producers, and the audience loved it. *Copacabana* is no great noteworthy artistic achievement, but it will make a lot of money and [is] a vindication of my determination to veer slightly away from the old character. I have some other movie plans brewing and will tell you about them when I see you.

I hope you will be able to live with us at the Shufros [*sic*]. I don't remember whether I wrote you that he had volunteered to let us use his apartment, as most of the time I will be in New York he will be in Florida with his family.

At any rate, give all your suitors my best and let me know what shows you haven't seen so I can get you seats for them. If some of those you have seen you want to see again, that too can be arranged.

Love and kisses and I hope you are all better by now. I am glad you liked the lingerie. You can give me a style show when I arrive, in a nice way of course.

*Your Padre*

# JOHN STEINBECK *to his son Thom*

*Born in August 1944, Thom was the older of John Steinbeck's two sons (John was born two years later). Their mother was Steinbeck's second wife, Gwendolyn. At the time he wrote the following letter, Steinbeck had been married eight years to his third wife, Elaine. This was to be his last, and most enduring, union. "I know your feeling," he tells Thom, "because I have it and I am glad you have it."*

◆ ◆ ◆

*[New York]*
*November 10, 1958*

Dear Thom:

We had your letter this morning. I will answer it from my point of view and of course Elaine will from hers.

First—if you are in love—that's a good thing—that's about the best thing that can happen to anyone. Don't let anyone make it small or light to you.

Second—There are several kinds of love. One is a selfish, mean, grasping, egotistic thing which uses love for self-importance. This is the ugly and crippling kind. The other is an outpouring of everything good in you—of kindness, and consideration and respect—not only the social respect of manners but the greater respect which is recognition of another person as unique and valuable. The first kind can make you sick and small and weak but the second can release in you strength, and courage and goodness and even wisdom you didn't know you had.

You say this is not puppy love. If you feel so deeply—of course it isn't puppy love.

But I don't think you were asking me what you feel. You know that better than anyone. What you wanted me to help you with is what to do about it—and that I can tell you.

Glory in it for one thing and be very glad and grateful for it.

The object of love is the best and most beautiful. Try to live up to it.

If you love someone—there is no possible harm in saying so —only you must remember that some people are very shy and sometimes the saying must take that shyness into consideration.

Girls have a way of knowing or feeling what you feel, but they usually like to hear it also.

It sometimes happens that what you feel is not returned for one reason or another—but that does not make your feeling less valuable and good.

Lastly, I know your feeling because I have it and I am glad you have it.

We will be glad to meet Susan. She will be very welcome. But Elaine will make all such arrangements because that is her province and she will be very glad to. She knows about love too and maybe she can give you more help than I can.

And don't worry about losing. If it is right, it happens—The main thing is not to hurry. Nothing good gets away.

*Love*
*Fa*

# On Living and
# Miscellaneous Matters

# FATHER JAMES HAROLD FLYE
## *to James Agee*

---

*In the summer of 1919, James Agee's family took a cottage at St. Andrews, a school for boys in Tennessee. The family consisted of his recently widowed mother, nine-year-old James Rufus, and his sister, Emma. Also living on the school grounds was a St. Andrews teacher, Father James Harold Flye. He was one of the first people James Agee met in his new home, and he became for the boy a teacher, spiritual adviser, foster father, and lifelong friend.*

*Agee went on to attend Phillips Exeter Academy and Harvard, to write film reviews for* Time *and* The Nation, *and to coauthor, with Walker Evans,* Let Us Now Praise Famous Men. *He also cowrote the screenplay for the movie* The African Queen, *among other works.*

*Father Flye and Agee corresponded throughout the latter's life, indeed right up to his death. Agee died on May 16, 1955, at age forty-five; his last letter to Flye was dated May 11 (it was found, by Flye himself, on the mantelpiece in Agee's house). "Nothing much to report," Agee wrote. "I feel, in general, as if I were dying."*

*Agee's only novel,* A Death in the Family, *which dramatizes the events surrounding his father's death, was published posthumously and won the 1958 Pulitzer Prize.*

◆ ◆ ◆

*St. Andrews, Tennessee*
*May 23, 1938*

*Dear Rufus:*

I am sorry for having let so long a time pass since receiving your letter—a time during which, to be sure, you have been in my thoughts a great deal. I wanted to write you a real letter, but for me who compose[s] with extreme slowness, that is usually a matter of some hours, and I found it hard to get a favorable time. What I thought of daily and should have done was to send you at once a few lines saying that I would write at length later but wanted to assure you under any circumstances and at all times of my great affection and care for you always.

I don't know that even now I need say any more than that. Each person's life is a problem with which he may, to be sure, get help, but which he himself, not someone else, must ultimately work out. There are some things about human life and nature and problems which I think I know. I myself have been helped by the wisdom of others, given either personally or through books. I do believe that if certain things could be said to us, certain considerations presented by wise and trusted friends just at the right time, it would often help us more than we could ever express or even know. You may know the poem "Debts," by Jessie B. Rittenhouse, beginning

> My debt to you, Beloved,
> Is one I cannot pay
> In any coin of any realm
> On any reckoning day;

What is needed may be encouragement, a word of understanding, perhaps just certain information. I have often wished I might be able thus to help someone in such need, some young person perhaps. But the person in question doesn't know what he needs, doesn't know that he might be helped, or doesn't know whom to speak with, or is too shy to be frank; or perhaps a wise and trusted counsellor is not at hand, or what is said is not heeded. Much that one may know simply cannot be handed on to another. And then one isn't always sure, himself. I hold different views on certain subjects now from what I did when I graduated from college, and further time may see other modifications. I believe I am in general wiser, of broader understanding, now than I was twenty-five years ago, but am conscious of ignorance and limitations. You would understand, then, from what I have said and from how you know I would feel, that I realize that your own life and problems are matters for you to work out; and in every effort to do this you have my sympathy and affection always. Life is difficult sometimes; though I must say I have never found it so hard to tell what was right *for me* to do as to think what . . . might be right for someone else to do under certain imagined circumstances. But after all, it is my life for which I am responsible, and I somehow imagine that for most persons the question "What is the right thing for me to do?" is likely to be easier than the one "What would be the right thing for someone else to do under such and such circumstances?" Life is often easier to live than to understand. And on this basis countless human beings have steadily carried heavy loads, have been brave and honorable and endured through much tribulation.

What I most want to say to you, however, is to tell you of my constant feeling of trust and understanding between us, and of my sympathy and appreciation and love for you always and also a word of encouragement. You have gone through some difficult and painful times. You have of course at various times made mistakes. At times, like all of us, you may have waywardness and weakness to regret, but from the time I first knew you I have seen in you some exceedingly fine things—a compassionate, tender heart, the capacity for understanding, for written expression, for high thoughts and noble living. With all my heart I wish for you the sort of life and achievement embodying your real ideal. I think of you daily.

> *Yours as ever,*
> *Father Flye*

# W. H. AUDEN *to his godson Philip Spender*

*Poet Wystan Hugh Auden (1907–1973) had no children of his own. He wrote the following poem, "Epistle to a Godson," for Philip Spender, son of the poet Stephen, who was a friend of Auden's from their student days at Oxford.*

◆ ◆ ◆

*April 1969*

DEAR PHILIP: "Thank God for boozy godfathers"
you wrote in our guest-book, which was flattering:
    though I've reached the years when discretion
    calls for a yearly medical check-up,

who am I to avouch for any Christian
baby, far less offer ghostly platitudes
    to a young man? In yester times it
    was different: the old could still be helpful

when they could nicely envisage the future
as a named and settled landscape their children
    would make the same sense of as they did,
    laughing and weeping at the same stories.

Then sheep and goats were easy to recognize,
local fauna: good meant Giles the shoemaker
    taking care of the village ninny,
    evil Count ffoulkes who in his tall donjon

indulged in sinister eccentricities.
But *I speak from experience*, how could I
    say that to you, who can't remember
    when everyone travelled by railway,

and the poor were what they were used to being,
the creators of wealth not, as now they are,
    an expensive nuisance? (Nobody
    has dared suggest gassing them, but someone

surely will.) You don't need me to tell you what's
going on: the ochlocratic media,
    joint with under-the-dryer gossip,
    process and vent without intermission

all to-day's ugly secrets. Imageable
no longer, a featureless anonymous
    threat from behind, to-morrow has us
    gallowed shitless: if what is to happen

occurs according to what Thucydides
defined as "human", we've had it, are in for
    a disaster that no four-letter
    words will tardy. I've beheld in nightmares

(who hasn't?) likely abominations: seething
behavioral sinks, the Muses scuttering,
    smelly, from eutrophied Helicon,
    the Witches' Sabbath on Garbage Mountain,

Herod's genetic engineers commanded
to modify the Innocents. By then, with
   any luck, the tangible Me should
   be mineral, too set in my habits

to distinguish light from darkness, and valued
in current prices at three-dollars-fifty:
   but you might well be there, if what is
   ripely is not promptly done. Yet who can

issue proper instructions? Not, certainly,
our global Archons, whose top-lofty slogans
   are as off the beam as their syntax
   is vague: (they would be figures of fun, if

very clever little boys had not found it
amusing to build devices for them, more
   apt at disassembly than any
   old fire-spewing theogonic monster.)

To be responsible for the happiness
of the Universe is not a sinecure:
   in elite lands your generation
   may be called to opt for a discipline

that out-peers the monks, a Way of obedience,
poverty and—good grief!—perhaps chastity,
   yet in this world's ill-weathered open,
   a stern venture pre-figured in folk-tales

as the Quest Perilous. For such wayfarers,
what should we write to give them the nourishment,
   warmth and shelter they'll be in need of?
   Nothing obscene or unpleasant: only

the unscarred overfed enjoy Calvary
as a verbal event. Nor satiric: no
   scorn will ashame the Adversary.
   Nor shoddily made: to give a stunning

display of concinnity and elegance
is the least we can do, and its dominant
   mood should be that of a Carnival.
   Let us hymn the small but journal wonders

of Nature and of households, and then finish
on a serio-comic note with legends
   of ultimate eucatastrophe,
   regeneration beyond the waters.

But perhaps you think poems are as foolish
as most poets, and would rather spend your spare
   moments romping around in Cantor's
   logical paradise, or beseeching

such knotty points as *Can we hang a robber
who is not there?* or *What is the color of
   the number Three?* Why not? All pleasures
   come from God. Since I *am* your godfather,

I'll close this letter with some worldly maxims:

*Be glad your being is unnecessary,*
*    then turn your toes out as you walk, dear,*
*    and remember who you are, a Spender.*

# BOB TEAGUE *to his son Adam*

*Dear Adam the New Adult:*

I have been meaning for some time to warn you about a subtle array of intellectual snares and pitfalls. Beyond childhood, you now are an unprotected species. Missteps can ruin your life. With all the printed maps and oral directions that you have been given up to now, you may feel quite prepared. I doubt that you are.

Lesson No. 1: Your maps include some miscalculations drawn by The Three Stooges. Almost every avenue, fast lane, and alley is either mislabeled or carries no label at all. You therefore must proceed at risk, my son. Don't trust any sign that says THIS IS THE ONLY WAY TO GO. Look for an alternate route that might serve you better.

Lesson No. 2: It is human to rely on one's own perceptions. Still, you would be wise to stop well short of ruling out every concept that challenges yours.

Lesson No. 3: Life and contradictions are synonymous. Sure, trying to live with contradictions can drive you bonkers. I can assure you, however, that you won't have any choice on that issue. In this higgledy-piggledy world of uncertainties, going bonkers to some degree is de rigueur. Besides, you will learn, to your advantage, that once your enemies are convinced you are crazy, they will be more inclined to leave you alone. Contradictions lend a certain yin-yang symmetry to all that we learn and experience.

Lesson No. 4: A crazy person with talent, money, or power is readily accepted as an eccentric.

Lesson No. 5: In addition to your maps, a whopping percentage of almost everything else that matters will also come packaged deceptively. Why? There is a long tradition among us foolish mortals to euphemize our errors, crimes, and fears. One shameful example was the advice of a White House aide, [Daniel] Patrick Moynihan, several years ago on the race problem. When the president asked what course his administration should take, the future New York senator coined a classic contradiction in two words: "Benign neglect." You probably were too young to notice when it happened, but Moynihan's euphemism became official policy.

Lesson No. 6: Before accepting or rejecting any label, consider who or what may be behind it. Punch up the suspect's rap sheet on your mental computer terminal. More often than not you will discover unsanitary self-saving motives. Reaganomics, for instance, has meant defining catsup as a vegetable when given to the poor. "Plea bargaining," as you know, means letting criminal parasites off with milder punishment than they deserve. In TV news, "live coverage" often means that the on-camera reporter is live, but the story is shown and told on videotape that had been shot and edited several hours earlier.

Lesson No. 7: Be especially wary of proposed quick fixes with mesmerizing labels like "open enrollment" or "community control." By lowering college admission standards to a militant black flag years ago, the liberal establishment created another mockery: A horde of illegitimate minority graduates, many of whom went on to become underachievers in various positions over their heads. They consistently "axed" the wrong questions and caused embarrassments to colleagues and employers, yet they were protected by civil rights directives. Lately, responsible educators have decided to go with a second opinion: What a stupid experiment that had been. Students who had failed to finish high school simply didn't belong in college. . . .

Lesson No. 8: Start compiling your own list of euphemistic labels. The validity of your thinking and the quality of your life will improve immeasurably when you begin to make a conscious daily effort to call this, that, and whatever by its right name.